# THE INTERNATIONAL PARTY COOKBOOK

# THE INTERNATIONAL PARTY COOKBOOK

by Rae Lindsay

DRAKE PUBLISHERS INC. NEW YORK

Published in 1973 by
Drake Publishers Inc.
381 Park Avenue South
New York, N.Y. 10016


© Rae Lindsay, 1973




Library of Congress Cataloging in Publication Data
Lindsay, Rae.
    International party cookbook

    1. Entertaining.    2. Cookery, International.
I. Title.
TX731.L5          641.5'68          73-4343
ISBN 0-87749-495-9




Printed in the United States of America

# TABLE OF CONTENTS

1791227

## BUFFETS, COCKTAIL PARTIES, SPECIAL OCCASIONS

to Alex, for inspiration, encouragement
and above all, patience
and Maria, Sandy and Robbie, my
taste-testers

special thanks to Mom, Camey, Linda, Joan, Karlene, Anita;
and Bob (of Bobanell's Liquors), and Tom, Andy and Pat (of
T & A Meats).

# INTRODUCTION

An international cook-book is a little like a trip around the world in 80 days—there's only so much that can be covered! A quick dip into Russian lenten customs and it's over to the South Seas to enjoy a luau.

Despite the whirl-wind tour, you come to realize as never before the wonderful universality of celebrations and culinary approaches. One can see how very much alike we all are, especially when it involves the world's favorite pastime—eating.

A few of the many examples that come to mind: pancakes are truly universal with Blintzes, Bliny, Crepes, Manicotti, Tortillas, Spring Rolls et al. The Scots, the Swiss, Americans, Russians, Germans and Brazilians all have their own version (very similar, too) of Pickled Eggs. In London you enjoy Roast Beef with Yorkshire Pudding, and in Vienna you have the same dish with Meltz, a popover affair.

Order Egg Drop Soup in China, Stracciatella in Rome, and Warfel in Vienna and you'll enjoy more or less the same tasty soup. English cookery books talk about Beef Olives—actually twins to Roladin, Roulades, the Swedish Kalvrulader, the Italian Braccioli and the American "bird." Peruvians dig a circular hole to prepare a "pachamanca," Mexicans call it a "barbacoa," Polynesians have an underground "imu," and Texans, of course, have their "barbecue."

The sociological aspects of food around the world are fascinating, but not the main purpose of this book. My aim in writing *The International Party Cookbook* was to provide the details for twenty unusual and internationally traditional parties. This is a guide to entertaining, with ideas for attractive settings, authentic customs and traditions, and above all, the recipes for a delicious array of food.

Because I believe wholeheartedly that the hostess should be with the guests and not in the kitchen, most of the recipes are do-ahead. This stress on "be prepared" has led to eliminating certain specialties which require close attention just before serving, or which can't with good results be done ahead.

While not a "gourmet" cookbook (a term I always find slightly pretentious), there's a lot of material here for the adventurous (and energetic) cook. The recipes incorporate convenience foods only when there's no sacrifice to taste or when the real thing (such as puff pastry) requires special expertise.

I happen to disagree with the idea that you shouldn't try out new recipes on guests. If you don't experiment then, when will you? And how much more gratifying to work hard at a splendid Smörgåsbord than to set out tried-and-true "store-bought" hors d'oeuvres. (Actually, the recipes, if followed accurately, should provide no real problems. All have been carefully tested for preparation, taste, and appearance.)

The book also ends the dilemma of "What shall I serve with what?" Instead of harried, random choosing from any number of sources, you can select a coordinated menu that carries out an entertaining theme. In addition, costs for all parties are detailed at the end of each chapter so the hostess can determine approximately how much a particular event will cost in advance. (No more Monday morning quarterbacking that "we spent too much.") The plans do *not* cover entertaining "on a budget"; my theory is: invite fewer people and serve better food. And in some instances (especially the larger parties) you can invite *more* people for roughly the same amount of money.

Most of all, the parties are fun. Entertaining with an international accent is rather like an open-end ticket for a trip around the world. So, as you travel, be my guest!

Rae Lindsay

# Brunch-Lunch-Coffee

## Make Merry at a New Orleans Creole Brunch . . . for 12–16 Jazz Fans

The United States has a dozen or so distinct regional cuisines, all reflecting the culture (as well as the locally available food) of the people who settled in various parts of the country.

Perhaps the most unique style of cooking is Creole, based on so many different influences: African, from the slaves who did the cooking; French, from the people, both aristocrats and peasants, who settled the area and named the city for the Duc d'Orleans; peppery Spanish spicing, added during the short time that Spain controlled the area; Acadian, from the Canadian emigrants (remember Evangeline?); and finally, secrets of herbs and spices from the Choctaw Indians. And, of course, the new land offered an abundance of fish; succulent, tropical fruit and vegetables; spices, herbs, beans, and rice.

But Creole cooking is more than an amalgam of these influences. There's something about Louisiana, and, in fact, New Orleans, that adds a special panache, the little extra fillip that makes for spectacular dining. The Creole philosophy is that eating should be a pleasure, not a task to hurry through. A study of old menus shows that breakfast was a five or six course affair, lunch stretched to eight or nine courses, and dinner —a true groaning board!

It was quality, not quantity, that mattered, of course; what the Creoles called "bonne bouches"—good mouthfuls. After the first influence of the 18th century French immigrants, the Spaniards came, bringing their penchant for hotter, more pungent seasonings. (Did you know that Tabasco Sauce is manufactured in Louisiana and that the pepper mash takes three years to mellow before it's blended with vinegar, bottled, and finally finds its way into your Bloody Mary?) The French returned in the 19th century: many noted chefs, valuing their heads, left France in a hurry. It must also be noted that there was a certain paucity of employers in guillotine-happy Paris. With the advent of the *toque blanche* crew, Creole cooking got a good dash of haute cuisine!

Aside from the melting pot, Creole culture, the Crescent City is the birthplace of America's original, uniquely indigenous form of music: jazz.

Like its culinary counterpart, jazz evolved from many sources. It was the freed slaves who heard a different drummer and developed this special music by blending African rhythms, European harmony, and melodic ideas from both continents. They took a little from ragtime piano, a lot from Negro work songs, Creole songs, religious hymns, the music of marching bands and minstrel shows . . . even funeral rhythms. The result was memorable.

What better way to pay tribute to New Orleans and score points for yourself as a knowledgeable hostess than to give a New Orleans brunch for jazz fans.

The music should be as authentic (and early) as you can beg, borrow or steal. Your local public library is a good source for the borrowing. Or, if you can collect a group of real jazz buffs as guests, ask them to bring their records to share. Some of the early names to remember include Louis Armstrong, the most famous exponent of the Basin Street-Bourbon Street-Rampart Street jazz; Freddie Keppard's Olympia Band; Kid Ory's Creole Jazz Band; the Eagle Band; King Oliver's Creole Jazz Band (with Louis Armstrong on second cornet, back in the early 20's), the New Orleans Rhythm Kings, and the Fletcher Henderson Band, not New Orleans based but with whom Armstrong played in the mid-20's, helping to make it the first of the big jazz bands. (Incidentally, by way of trivia tid-bits, the term jazz was first applied to a group of New Orleans musicians who were playing in Chicago in 1916. It came from the French verb "jaser", meaning "to babble." From being known as "jass" music, eventually the word became JAZZ!)

Now that you have your jazzy background, back to the "bonne bouches" or good mouthfuls. The food planned for your New Orleans brunch is purposely "proletarian." Although you might find some of the items on the menu at Brennan's, Antoine's, Arnaud's and other famous New Orleans restaurants, I've tried to provide a cross-section of Creole cooking which can, for the most part, be prepared beforehand. Oysters Rockefeller, for example, is a typical Crescent City dish (and a lovely one at that), but you have to be right there in the kitchen to cook it . . . and that's not my idea of party giving.

So, get a new needle for the stereo, select a guest roster that really does like jazz, call your fish market and order scads of seafood . . . and enjoy a Creole brunch on an upcoming Sunday. Here's the menu:

# New Orleans Creole Brunch for 12–16

Sazeracs                                     Creole Old-Fashioneds

## Appetizers

Pâté de Crevettes    Canapés de Crabes    Anchoix a L'Oeufs
(shrimp pâté)    (crabmeat canapés)  (anchovies and eggs)

## Main Course

Shrimp Gumbo                              Creole Jambalaya

Steamed Rice

Louisiana Salad                              French Bread

## Desserts

Rice Calas                        Tarte de Coco à la Creole
(rice fritters)                        (creole coconut pie)

Pralines                                  Fresh Fruit

Café Brûlot Diabolique

# *Sazerac Cocktails*

**For 12 cocktails:**

4½ cups bourbon

6 teaspoons extra-fine sugar

1 teaspoon angostura bitters

1 teaspoon pernod

ice cubes

strips of lemon peel

**EARLY ON DAY OF PARTY:**

1. Add bourbon, sugar, bitters, and pernod to a glass jar. Shake several times. Chill.

**AT PARTY TIME:**

1. Shake Sazerac mix well. Place two ice cubes in 12 old-fashioned glasses; add Sazerac mix and a strip of lemon peel.

# *Creole Old-Fashioneds*

**For 12 Old-Fashioneds:**

4½ cups bourbon or scotch

6 teaspoons extra fine sugar

1 tablespoon lemon juice

ice cubes

orange slices

maraschino cherries

strips of lemon peel

**EARLY ON DAY OF PARTY:**

1. Add bourbon or scotch, sugar and lemon juice to glass jar. Shake well; refrigerate.

**AT PARTY TIME:**

1. Shake old-fashioned mix well. Add 2 ice cubes to 12 old-fashioned glasses, pour in the old-fashioned mix. Add a slice of orange and a cherry, twist a strip of lemon peel over the drink to release oil and add to drink.

# Appetizers

Unlike the custom in most American homes, in old-time Creole cuisine, canapés were served for breakfast, as well as at lunch or dinner. The word "canapé" literally means a bed or couch to rest the remainder of the meal on.

## Pâté De Crevettes
### (Shrimp pâté)

4 tablespoons pernod
juice of ½ lemon
1 pound cooked shrimp,
   shelled and deveined
½ teaspoon ground mace
dash of tabasco

1 teaspoon dijon or similar
   mustard
1 stick butter at room
   temperature
1 teaspoon salt
freshly ground black pepper

**DAY BEFORE PARTY:**
1. Add pernod, lemon juice, shrimp and seasonings except salt and pepper to blender container. Blend by turning motor on and off and stirring with a spoon (motor *off*, of course) only until mixture is coarsely chopped.
2. Stir softened butter into shrimp mixture; add salt and pepper to taste and blend well. Place in serving bowl or mold; refrigerate. Serve with toast rounds or triangles.

## Canapés de Crabes
### (Crab Canapés)

18 thin slices white bread

1 8-ounce package cream

5 tablespoons melted butter
1 7-ounce can crabmeat,
  well-drained and flaked

cheese, at room
  temperature
¼ cup ketchup
1 teaspoon grated onion
capers for garnish

**EARLY ON DAY OF PARTY:**
1. Toast bread, then cut 4 rounds from each slice with 1¼"
cookie cutter. Brush top side of rounds lightly with melted
butter.
2. Mix remaining ingredients (except capers) together until
fluffy. Drop a teaspoon or so of filling in a mound on each
round. Garnish with drained capers.
3. Cover with plastic wrap and refrigerate until party time.

# Anchoix à L'Oeufs
## (Anchovies with Eggs)

3 small tins of rolled anchovies, packed in oil, well drained
3 hard boiled eggs, peeled and sliced
melba or other rounds

**EARLY ON DAY OF PARTY:**
1. Place a slice of egg on each toast round and top with an
anchovy fillet. Sprinkle with paprika. Cover with plastic wrap
and refrigerate until party time.

**AT PARTY TIME:**
1. Arrange Anchoix à l'oeufs canapés on tray with Crab canapés.

# Shrimp Gumbo

Gumbo is as important to Creole cooking as pasta is to Italian cuisine. This soup-stew-meal-in-a-dish was a happy accident that became a real touchstone of New Orleans fare.

There are many, many variations of the dish: vegetable gumbos, seafood gumbos, chicken or turkey gumbos, and even combinations of seafood and poultry. Gumbo, also spelled gombo was created from the use of filé, the powdered sassafras used by the Choctaw Indians for medicinal purposes. Not wanting to give short shrift to a good thing, Creole cooks also devised gumbos using okra, instead of filé, as a thickener. The rule to remember, however, is never use filé and okra in the same recipe. You'll have one gluey mess!

## Shrimp Gumbo

1 stick butter
6 tablespoons flour
3 large onions, chopped
 (about 3 cups)  ·
2 cloves garlic, minced
2 1-pound, 12-ounce cans of
 tomatoes
2 cans condensed chicken
 broth
4 cups water
2 teaspoons salt
2 tablespoons Worcester-
 shire sauce
½ teaspoon tabasco sauce
1 bay leaf
4 or 5 sprigs parsley
1 teaspoon thyme
1 16-ounce box of converted
 rice. (2 cups raw rice)
2 teaspoons salt
2 tablespoons butter
2 pounds of *small*, raw,
 shelled, deveined shrimp
2 pints fresh oysters or
 about 5 7-ounce cans
 oysters
4 tablespoons filé powder

17

**DAY BEFORE PARTY:**
1. Make a roux (the basic flavor base for many Creole—and French—dishes) by melting the butter in a heavy skillet and stirring in the flour. Cook, stirring constantly, over low heat until flour turns brown, about 15 minutes.
2. Add onions and garlic. Cook, stirring frequently, until onions and garlic are soft, about 10 minutes. Add tomatoes, chicken broth, water, salt, Worcestershire sauce, tabasco, bay leaf, parsley and thyme. Cover skillet.
3. Simmer 15 minutes to develop flavors.
4. Refrigerate overnight.

**AT PARTY TIME:**
1. One hour before serving remove gumbo from refrigerator.
2. 30 minutes before serving, bring 4-¾ cups water to a boil; add 2 cups raw rice plus 2 teaspoons salt and 2 tablespoons butter. Cover tightly and cook over low heat until all water is absorbed (25 minutes).
3. 10 minutes before serving, add shrimp and oysters with their juice to gumbo. Continue cooking until oysters are curled (about 7 minutes).
4. Sprinkle filé powder into gumbo and stir well to thicken broth. Serve immediately with cooked rice as accompaniment.

# Creole Jambalaya

2 chicken breasts, split
  (4 pieces)
4 cups of water, seasoned
  with salt and pepper
4 tablespoons oil
2 cups finely chopped onions
2 cups chopped green pepper

2 #2 cans tomatoes (5 cups)
2 cups raw white rice
3 cups chicken broth
1 teaspoon thyme
2 tablespoons chopped
  parsley
½ teaspoon chili powder

3 cloves garlic, finely minced
1 cup diced, cooked ham
16 small pork sausages cut
  in ¾" pieces

freshly ground black pepper
  to taste
2 teaspoons salt

**DAY BEFORE PARTY:**
1. Cook chicken in 4 cups water seasoned with salt and pepper for about 30 minutes until chicken is tender. Drain chicken; reserve broth.
2. Preheat oven to 350°.
3. Heat oil in skillet and add onion, green pepper and garlic. Cook slowly, stirring, until onion and pepper are soft. Add the cooked chicken, ham and sausage and cook 5 minutes.
4. Add tomatoes with their liquid, rice, 3 cups of the reserved chicken broth, and spices. Turn into ovenproof casserole. Cover and bake until rice is almost tender, about one hour. Cool to room temperature.
5. Refrigerate, covered, overnight.

**DAY OF PARTY:**
1. Remove casserole from refrigerator one hour before serving.
2. Preheat oven to 350°.
3. Reheat casserole for 15–20 minutes or until rice is tender and ingredients are well heated.

## Louisiana Salad

*Salad:*

2 heads of lettuce, torn
3 cucumbers, pared and
  thinly sliced
½ cup of small pickled
  onions

*Dressing:*

⅔ cup olive oil
¼ cup cider vinegar
3 teaspoons prepared
  mustard
2 hard-boiled egg yolks,
  well mashed
Salt and pepper to taste

**EARLY ON DAY OF PARTY:**
1. Prepare salad vegetables.
2. Mix dressing ingredients in a glass jar and shake well.

**AT PARTY TIME:**
1. Toss lettuce, cucumbers, and onions with prepared dressing. Test for salt and pepper and serve.

# Tarte De Coco À La Creole
## (Creole Coconut Pie)

1½ cups sugar
¾ cup cornstarch
½ teaspoon salt
4½ cups hot milk
5 egg yolks, beaten
2 tablespoons butter

¼ cup bourbon
3 cups coconut
11-inch baked pie shell
1 cup heavy cream, whipped
   with 1 teaspoon sugar

**DAY BEFORE PARTY:**
1. Combine sugar, cornstarch and salt; gradually add to hot milk in large saucepan, stirring until smooth. Bring to boil, stirring over medium heat. Boil 2 minutes. Remove from stove.
2. Stir half of hot mixture into egg yolks, then combine egg mixture with milk mixture. Add butter. Cook, stirring over low heat until custard boils and mounds from the spoon. About 2 minutes.
3. Turn into a bowl; stir in bourbon and 1½ cups coconut. Place plastic wrap or waxed paper on top of filling so it doesn't form

a "skin." Refrigerate 2 hours.
4. Turn into prepared pie shell. Refrigerate overnight.
5. Spread remaining coconut on cookie sheet. Place under broiler briefly to toast. Set aside.

**AT PARTY TIME:**
1. Spread whipped cream over pie; top with toasted coconut. Serve cold.

# *Rice Calas*
## *(Rice Fritters)*

These fritters used to be sold piping hot, wrapped in a clean towel by Creole Negro women on the streets of Vieux Carré. Most were prepared by the women at home, but some were cooked over charcoal stoves on busy street corners. As the Creole women cried "belle calas tout chaud," wealthier residents of the French Quarter would wake up and face the world with a cup of café au lait and these delightful calas.

*For 20 Calas:*

½ cup uncooked rice
1½ cups boiling water
½ package yeast
2 tablespoons warm water
3 eggs, well beaten
¼ cup sugar

½ teaspoon salt
⅛ teaspoon nutmeg
¼ cup sifted flour
  (approximately)
oil for deep frying
confectioners sugar

**NIGHT BEFORE PARTY:**
1. Add rice to boiling water. Simmer, covered, until rice is very tender and water is absorbed. About 25 minutes. Mash rice

and cool.

2. Dissolve yeast in warm water. Add to rice; mix thoroughly. Cover with a dish cloth. Let rise in warm place overnight.

**EARLY ON DAY OF PARTY:**

1. Add eggs, sugar, salt and nutmeg to rice and blend. Add the flour a little at a time to make a thick batter. Cover. Let rise in warm place 20 minutes.

2. Heat oil in deep fryer or electric frying pan to 360°. Drop batter by tablespoonsful into oil (don't crowd). Fry until golden brown. Drain on paper towels. Sprinkle with confectioners sugar.

3. Wrap in towel. At serving time, re-warm on electric hot tray or in 150° oven.

# *Pralines*

This candied concoction was a French inspiration, originally made with almonds. In Louisiana, those with sweet teeth for nuts used sugared pecans instead which grow wild in the area.

4½ cups light brown sugar        2 tablespoons butter
1 cup warm water                 1 pound pecans

**DAY BEFORE PARTY:**

1. Combine sugar, water, and butter. Boil over medium heat, stirring, until a small amount of mixture forms a soft ball in cold water (236° on candy thermometer). Remove from heat, stir in pecan halves, and cool to lukewarm (110°, or until cool enough to comfortably touch the bottom of the pan with your hand). While mixture is cooling, do not stir.

2. When lukewarm, beat candy with a spoon for a minute or

two. Drop by tablespoons onto lightly greased serving dish. (Makes about 50–60 pralines.)

## *Café Brûlot Diabolique*

A traditional and spectacular finale at Antoine's and other famous New Orleans restaurants:

| | |
|---|---|
| 2 1-inch sticks cinnamon | 6 lumps sugar |
| 16 whole cloves | 6 jiggers brandy |
| peel of 2 lemons, cut thin | 6 cups strong coffee (use French Market type) |

**AT PARTY TIME:**
1. Place cinnamon, cloves, lemon peel and sugar in a chafing dish.
2. Heat brandy in a large ladle. Ignite the brandy and pour over ingredients in chafing dish until sugar is dissolved.
3. Gradually add coffee, ladling mixture in chafing dish until flames fade. Serve immediately. (Makes 16 small cups.)

## *Approximate Expenses for New Orleans Brunch for 12–16 Jazz Fans:*

| | |
|---|---|
| $ 8.10 | Sazeracs |
| 8.10 | Creole Old-Fashioneds |
| 4.55 | Pâté de Crevettes   (shrimp pâté) |
| 2.45 | Canapés de Crabes (crab meat canapés) |

| | |
|---|---|
| 2.15 | Anchoix à l'oeufs (anchovies and eggs) |
| 10.65 | Shrimp Gumbo |
| 4.95 | Creole Jambalaya |
| .50 | Steamed Rice |
| 2.30 | Louisiana Salad |
| 1.00 | French Bread (2 loaves) |
| .20 | butter |
| .85 | Rice Calas |
| 2.55 | Creole Coconut Pie |
| 2.05 | Pralines |
| 2.50 | Fresh Fruit |
| 3.30 | Café Brûlot Diabolique |
| $56.20 | |

$3.50 a person is the realistic estimate for this full-fledged brunch for 12–16 guests.

# Ladies First at A Hollandse Koffietafel
## (Dutch Treat Luncheon)
## for 8 of the Girls

"Having the girls to lunch" used to call forth an image of very properly dressed ladies, white gloved, and hatted, politely sipping a sherry before delicately picking at chicken à la king.

Times have changed, and most of the ladies I know will arrive in sleek pant suits, enjoy a martini or Bloody Mary, and look forward to something a little different than the lady-like chicken dish.

So when you want to have your friends over for the sheer fun of it or before an afternoon of tennis or to plan some important committee work for your favorite public service activity, schedule a Dutch Treat luncheon, for girls only, but with some updated differences.

First off, scratch the sherry for a livelier beverage. Go all the way with Genever (also spelled Jenever), a beverage identified as Dutch gin which has very little in common with English gin aside from the name. Genever was originally sold in drug stores centuries ago as a medicinal drink invented by a dentist. It proved so popular that soon apothecaries were forming their own distilleries to provide the drink that obviously was not used for medicinal purposes alone.

Dutch Gin *cannot* be substituted for English gin in cocktails. It has a very distinct and malty aroma which doesn't take well to combination with other elements. There are many Dutch brands, but the main difference is between the "old" and the "young" varieties. The "old" is a little more oily and stronger, so when ordering Genever ask your liquor store to give you something "young." While it isn't the mildest aperitif, it's a great pick-up in reasonable quantities. (Limit your luncheon guests to two little brandy glasses or shot glasses of chilled Genever each . . . then serve lunch, QUICK!)

25

In Holland, lunch is called "Hollandse Koffietafel." The menu usually includes several cold dishes—salami, sausages, ham, roast beef, cheese, different breads, and one little warm dish, plus salad, capped with dessert and endless cups of coffee.

For our American version of Hollandse Koffietafel we pick up the idea of the warm dish, plus a fresh vegetable and salad. While our menu is typical, it's *atypical* of the luncheon specialties in fine Amsterdam restaurants. As in many countries, Continental eateries feature a few national dishes, but stress international food. To get the true feeling of a country you have to go into ordinary homes. In this sense, our Hollandse Koffietafel is authentic.

This should not be a buffet lunch, but a pleasant sit-down affair and don't forget to plan on extra coffee for the gab session after lunch. Then enjoy the festivities. As they say in Holland "Eet smakelijk" . . . good eating!

# Hollandse Koffietafel for 8

*Genever—Dutch Gin (chilled)*

## Appetizers

*Gevulde eieren*　　　　　　　　　　　　*Kassballetjes*
*(Stuffed Eggs)*　　　　　　　　　　　　*(Cheese Puffs)*

## Main Course

*Garnalen Croquetten Met Hollandaise Saus*
*(Shrimp Croquettes with Hollandaise Sauce)*

*Asperges Met Eieren*　　　　　　　　　*Tomatensla*
*(Asparagus with Egg Garnish)*　　　　*(Tomato Salad)*

*Small Pumpernickel or Rye Rolls–Sweet Butter*

## Dessert

*Citroenvla*　　　　　　　　　　　*Citron Spritz Koekjes*
*(Dutch Lemon Cream)*　　　　　*(Lemon Spritz Cookies)*

*Coffee*

# Gevulde Eieren

## (Stuffed Eggs)

8 eggs, hard-boiled and
  peeled
4 tablespoons butter,
  softened
½ clove garlic, chopped

2 anchovies, finely chopped
1 teaspoon capers
1 teaspoon chopped parsley
Mayonnaise (about ½ cup)

**EARLY ON DAY OF PARTY:**
1. Cut eggs in half carefully. Remove yolks and force through sieve into a bowl. Add butter, garlic, anchovies and capers. Blend well, add parsley and salt and pepper to taste.
2. Add mayonnaise, but don't make mixture too liquidy. If you want to be fancy, press the egg yolk mixture through a pastry bag with a rosette tube into the egg white halves. Chill before serving. Garnish with paprika or a few sprigs of parsley.

# Kassballetjes

## (Cheese Puffs)

3 tablespoons butter
5 tablespoons flour
1 cup milk, heated
1½ cups grated Edam or
  Gouda cheese

½ cup flour
3 egg yolks, beaten
1 teaspoon salt
¼ teaspoon pepper
3 egg whites, stiffly beaten
oil for deep frying

**DAY BEFORE PARTY:**
1. Melt butter, then stir in 5 tablespoons flour. Add hot milk all at once. Cook and stir sauce with wire whisk until smooth and thick. Add cheese and stir until melted.
2. Remove sauce from heat; blend in ½ cup flour, beaten egg yolks, salt and pepper. Gently fold in egg whites.
3. With small spoon, drop about a spoonful of mixture in hot fat. Let puff; then drain on absorbent paper. (About 60 puffs).
4. Cover and refrigerate overnight.

**AT PARTY TIME:**
1. Remove cheese puffs from refrigerator 1 hour before serving.
2. Reheat puffs briefly in 250° oven. Serve hot.

## *Garnalen Croquetten*
### *(Shrimp Croquettes)*

6 tablespoons butter
6 tablespoons flour
2 cups milk
4 cups raw shrimp, finely minced
2 tablespoons chopped parsley

1 teaspoon salt
½ teaspoon white pepper
1 teaspoon nutmeg
3 cups plain bread crumbs
2 eggs
Oil for deep frying

**DAY BEFORE PARTY:**
1. Melt butter. Remove from heat and blend in flour. Heat milk until bubbles form, then add all at once to butter-flour mixture, stirring with a wire whisk. Return to heat and cook for a few more minutes until sauce thickens. Add the shrimp, parsley, salt and pepper and nutmeg, then stir well. Spread about ½″ thick on a dish and refrigerate for 1 hour or until mixture is quite firm.

2. Using about 1 heaping tablespoon of the shrimp mixture, shape in round or elongated croquettes. Roll in bread crumbs. Continue shaping and rolling until mixture is used up. (24 small croquettes or 16 medium ones).
3. Beat eggs with 2 tablespoons water. Roll croquettes in egg mixture; then once more in bread crumbs. Cover and refrigerate overnight.
4. Fry croquettes in deep hot (375°) oil until brown. Drain on paper towels. Place in oven-proof serving dish. Cover. Set aside at room temperature.

**AT PARTY TIME:**
1. Preheat oven to 400°. Reheat croquettes for 10 minutes. Serve with Hollandaise sauce.

# *Hollandaise Saus*
## *(Hollandaise Sauce)*

What better and more authentic sauce to go over shrimp croquettes and asparagus than the nationally named favorite. Hollandaise sauce can be tricky, but if you use a blender, you'll pull it off without curdling.

| | |
|---|---|
| 1 cup butter | ½ teaspoon salt |
| 6 egg yolks | pinch cayenne pepper |
| 4 tablespoons lemon juice | |

**HALF AN HOUR BEFORE GUESTS ARRIVE:**
1. Melt butter in small saucepan until bubbly. Don't brown.
2. Place egg yolks, lemon juice, salt and cayenne in blender container. Cover. Turn motor on and off. Remove cover. Turn

motor to highest speed and add butter in a slow, steady stream. Turn off motor and sauce is done.

3. Keep warm by setting blender container in 2 inches of hot, *not boiling*, water.

## Asperges Met Eieren
### (Asparagus with Egg Garnish)

48 asparagus spears (about
4 pounds)
1 teaspoon salt
1 stick butter

½ cup fine bread crumbs
2 hard-cooked eggs, sieved
chopped parsley

**EARLY ON DAY OF PARTY:**
1. Snap off tough ends of asparagus, place in a large skillet with just enough boiling salted water to cover. Cover skillet and cook asparagus at low heat just until tender, about 12 minutes. Drain well, and gently. Store at room temperature.
2. In saucepan melt butter, add breadcrumbs and saute until lightly browned. Set aside at room temperature.

**AT SERVING TIME:**
1. Add a little water to skillet with asparagus. Reheat quickly.
2. Sprinkle buttered crumbs and any excess butter over hot asparagus; then sprinkle with sieved hard-cooked egg and chopped parsley.

## Tomatensla
### (Tomato Salad)

2 tablespoons oil

1 teaspoon sugar

2 teaspoons salt
1 teaspoon white pepper
2 teaspoons chopped onion

8 tomatoes, sliced
lettuce leaves
1 tablespoon chopped parsley

**EARLY ON DAY OF PARTY:**
1. Mix oil, salt, pepper, onion and sugar in a glass jar. Shake well.
2. On individual dishes, arrange sliced tomatoes on lettuce leaves. Refrigerate.

**AT SERVING TIME:**
1. Pour salad dressing over tomatoes. Sprinkle with chopped parsley.

# *Citroenvla*
# *(Dutch Lemon Cream)*

8 eggs, separated
1 cup sugar
Grated rind of 2 lemons

Juice of 4 lemons
1 cup dry vermouth

**DAY BEFORE PARTY:**
1. Beat egg yolks and sugar in top of double boiler until thick. Add lemon rind. Stir in lemon juice and wine. Cook mixture over hot (not boiling) water, beating constantly with rotary beater until mixture is thick and stiff. Cool overnight.

**AT SERVING TIME:**
1. One hour before party, beat egg whites until very stiff and fold gently into cream. Turn into sherbet glasses and chill. Serve with Lemon Spritz cookies.

# Citron Spritz Koekjes
## (Lemon Spritz Cookies)

1 cup butter
1 3-ounce package cream
  cheese
1 cup sugar
1 egg
1 tablespoon lemon juice
1 teaspoon grated lemon peel

2½ cups sifted all-purpose
  flour
1 teaspoon baking powder
lemon glaze, below
½ cup chopped almonds for
  garnish

**DAY BEFORE PARTY:**
1. Work butter and cream cheese in bowl until creamy. Add sugar and beat until light and fluffy. Add egg, lemon juice and lemon peel. Beat thoroughly.
2. Sift together flour and baking powder; add to butter mixture gradually and mix until smooth. Cover and chill 30 minutes.
3. Preheat oven to 375°. Put star plate in cookie press and fill press with dough. Force out 2 inch ribbons in the shape of an "S" onto cold, ungreased cookie sheets. Bake 10 to 12 minutes until edges are browned. Remove from sheets and cool on racks.
4. Dip ends of cookies in lemon glaze and then in chopped nuts. Place on waxed paper until glaze hardens. (48 cookies)
LEMON GLAZE: Combine 1 cup sifted confectioners sugar and 2 tablespoons lemon juice until smooth.

# Expenses for Dutch Treat Luncheon for 8:

$ 2.00    Genever
   .95    Gevulde Eieren (stuffed eggs)
  1.45    Kassballetjes (cheese puffs)

| | |
|---|---|
| 5.00 | Garnalen Croquetten met Hollandaise (shrimp croquettes) |
| 2.45 | Asperges met eieren (asparagus with eggs) |
| 1.20 | Tomatensla (tomato salad) |
| 1.20 | pumpernickel or rye rolls/butter |
| 1.50 | Citroenvla (lemon cream) |
| .80 | Citron Spritz Koekjes (cookies) |
| .75 | Coffee |
| $17.30 | |

$2.15 per person is all it takes to treat 8 of the girls to a Dutch Treat luncheon.

# Entertain Graciously at an Austrian Kaffeeklatsche— "Jause"—for 12

Austria was once the hub of the huge Hapsburg Empire, spreading east, west, north, and south from the focal point, glittering Vienna. Today, Austria is a small country about the size of Maine with a population close to New York City's.

Whatever the diminished glories of a once-fantastic empire, Austria still rates superlatives for its cuisine. In Vienna one can enjoy unusual soups (try "Hideg Meggyleves," cold sour cherry soup); luscious and waist-ruining dumplings ("leberknödel," liver dumplings or "kynuté ovocné Knedlíky," yeast fruit dumplings); succulent schnitzel, chicken paprikas, and dozens of varieties of boiled beef, "gekochtes Rindfleisch." But the one category of food most beloved by Viennese—and vistors to Vienna—has to be their pastries, always coupled with some form of "kaffe."

Coffee was actually introduced by the Turks who invaded Vienna in both 1529 and 1683. When they left Austria they left behind the talent for making and the appreciation of good strong coffee. Eventually the coffee addiction developed into the establishment of the "kaffeehaus." By the 19th Century, gathering at coffeehouses known for their brew and baked specialties became a way of life. Today, in any of the 800 coffeehouses in Vienna you can enjoy a cup of coffee in every shade from darkest brown (mokka) to palest "melange" (coffee with milk). Coffee is always served with a big bowl of "schlagobers," or whipped cream, on the side.

Schlagobers, affectionately nicknamed "schlag," is also a crucial accessory for any of the hundreds of pastries featured in the coffeehouses. In fact, between 3 and 5 in the afternoon, if you visit a kaffeehaus, you're expected to sample 2 or 3 pastries, always with some schlag as a final fillip.

It's no wonder that Viennese girls of all ages are described as being "mollig" or "voll-schank"—full-slim—an Austrian way of saying "pleasantly plump." (Viennese ladies, incidentally, are chivalrously addressed as "gnädigste, most gracious one!)

In addition to the kaffeehausen, more than 1500 pastry shops stack the odds against being skinny-slim in Vienna. These marvelously appealing bakeries produce desserts for those who opt for the domesticated version of afternoon coffee. This 4 o'clock interim, observed in many middle and upper class homes, is called a "Jause" (say "Yow-zeh") and is the occasion for a good old-fashioned gossip session, a practice that has universal popularity. To give a Jause at home, everything must be spectacularly elegant. Viennese women use their best lace tablecloths and set the dining room table with sparkling silver and a lush bouquet of fresh flowers. The featured food includes an array of attractively garnished Vorspiesen (appetizers) and the all-important torten, kuchen, strudeln, and other pastries, plus the coffee urn and mountainous bowls of schlag.

Some years ago, arranging a little Jause for a dozen or so friends didn't take much doing since the Viennese lady of the gay nineties had a rather easy life. After rising at 9:00 a.m. for a breakfast-in-bed of rolls, butter, jam and coffee, our lady would see the hairdresser or masseuse (who faithfully came to work off yesterday's schlag—an ever-losing battle). Then after the main meal of the day, "Mittagessen," she would have an hour's nap and prepare to play hostess at the gossip session, beautifully prepared by the resident cook and attendant maids.

Well, those days are gone—certainly for most Americans—but it still is a great deal of fun to collect your friends for patter and pastry, to celebrate a new baby, an engagement... or to plan a fund-raising activity, a political event.

In planning a Jause, the first thought might be to include strudel, which, is the most famous dessert that comes from Austria. Strudel was actually introduced to Austrians by way of Hungary, once part of the Empire, but the Hungarians got the idea from the Turks who are famous for their own baklava. I think we should leave strudel, delightful as it is, to those who are willing to put in the hours and hours of time necessary to perfect the technique of making strudel dough. The right flour and many hours of practice are crucial. It is possible to simulate strudel with phyllo pastry leaves, but it's not quite the same thing. Instead, find a good strudel store or Austrian-Hungarian restaurant and enjoy the "store-bought" versions of this delicacy.

Other Austrian pastries are easy enough to emulate for your own gossipy gathering. In our menu we've included the most famous torten of all, Sachertorte, a delightful, chocolatey concoction originally invented by Metternich's private chef, Franz Sacher, in 1832. For years afterwards Sachertorte was a specialité of the Hotel Sacher, run by the chef's descendents. Would you believe this airy goodie was even the subject of a law suit between the Hotel Sacher and the famous Demel's Pastry Shop as to which establishment had the right to advertise the "original" Sachertorte? The Hotel Sacher won, but to be fair both versions of the cake are delicious. We have included the Sacher's variation which is sliced and filled with apricot jam.

Sachertorte shares honors with three other glorious dessert pastries, plus "kaffe mit schlagobers" of course, and four appetizers which are mouth watering and eye-catching.

Here's the menu for your own elegant Jause. As the Viennese say before each meal: "Mahlzeit!" ... happy eating!

# Austrian Kaffeeklatsche ("Jause") for 12

## Vorspeisen (Appetizers)

Schinken-Spargelbrot
(Ham-Asparagus Canapés)

Crevettenbrot
(Shrimp Canapés)

Liptauer
(Cream Cheese Spread)

Russische Eier
(Russian Eggs)

Gumpoldkirschner Wine, chilled

## Torten (Cakes)

Sachertorte
(Chocolate Cake)

Haselnusstorte
(Hazelnut Cake)

Vanillekipferl
(Vanilla Crescents)

Schaumrolle
(Cream Rolls)

Schlagobers (Whipped Cream)

Kaffee (Coffee)

# Schinken-Spargelbrot
# (Ham-Asparagus Canapés)

Sweet butter, room
  temperature
12 slices party rye or 12
  slices white bread, crusts
  removed, trimmed to about
  3″ square
6 slices ham, cut in half or
  even thirds to fit bread
  neatly

12 cooked, chilled fresh or
  frozen asparagus spears
  (they should be dainty)
2 small tomatoes, cut in
  wedges
1 hard-boiled egg, thinly
  sliced
2 or 3 tablespoons
  mayonnaise
  parsley for garnish

**EARLY ON DAY OF PARTY:**
1. Lightly butter bread.
2. Cover bread with ham. Lay an asparagus spear diagonally
on top of ham. Place 1 piece of tomato on one side of asparagus,
a slice of egg on the other, a small dollop of mayonnaise on
center of asparagus, and a tiny leaf of parsley in the center.
3. Cover carefully with plastic wrap and refrigerate until serving
time. (Makes 12 canapés.)

# Crevettenbrot
# (Shrimp Canapé)

12 slices white bread,
  trimmed to about 3″ square
Mayonnaise
24 small cooked shrimp

1 hard-boiled egg, thinly
  sliced
24 capers

3 tomatoes, cut in wedge-
  shaped eighths

**EARLY ON DAY OF PARTY:**
1. Spread each slice of bread with thin coating of mayonnaise. Arrange 2 shrimp attractively on each slice. Then cut each egg slice and each tomato wedge in half and place around shrimp. Add a dollop of mayonnaise to center of canapé. Garnish with capers.
2. Cover carefully with plastic wrap and refrigerate until serving time. (Makes 12 canapés.)

# *Liptauer*
## *(Cream Cheese Spread)*

This cheese spread, one of Vienna's favorite appetizers, was originated in the town of Liptau, once part of the Austrian Empire, today a Czechoslovakian city.

1 pound cream cheese
  (2 8-ounce packages)
½ stick butter
1 teaspoon anchovy paste
½ teaspoon chopped capers
2 teaspoons prepared
  mustard
1 teaspoon caraway seeds,
  crushed

½ teaspoon salt
dash of pepper
2 tablespoons sweet paprika
4 tablespoons chopped
  chives
1 loaf of party pumpernickel
  bread

**DAY BEFORE PARTY:**
1. Cream the cheese and butter. Blend in anchovy paste, capers, mustard, caraway seeds, salt, pepper and 1 tablespoon of the paprika. Using a spatula, shape mixture into a cone on a serving plate.
2. Mix chives with remaining paprika. With fingers, pat chives-paprika mixture in several rows around cone. At base of cone, press leftover chives-paprika as a border.
3. Cover carefully with plastic wrap, using toothpicks to keep wrap away from cheese. Refrigerate. Serve cold with slices of party pumpernickel.

# *Russische Eier*
## *(Russian Eggs)*

| | |
|---|---|
| 6 hard-boiled eggs, peeled | 1 teaspoon chopped parsley |
| ½ cup mayonnaise | ¼ teaspoon anchovy paste |
| 1 teaspoon chopped dill pickle | 1 teaspoon chopped capers |
| 1 teaspoon minced onion | 2 ounces black caviar |

**EARLY ON DAY OF PARTY:**
1. Cut eggs in half lengthwise. Scoop out yolks and purée with fork. Mix with mayonnaise. Add pickle, onion, parsley, anchovy paste, capers. Mix to blend well.
2. Stuff into egg-white halves. Wrap carefully with plastic wrap; refrigerate.

**AT SERVING TIME:**
1. Garnish each egg with ½ teaspoon of caviar. (Makes 12)

# Sachertorte
# (Chocolate Cake)

1 6-ounce package semi-
  sweet chocolate chips
8 egg yolks
1 stick sweet butter, melted
1 teaspoon vanilla extract
10 egg whites
pinch of salt
¼ cup sugar
1 cup sifted all-purpose flour

3 ounces unsweetened
  chocolate, in small chunks
1 cup heavy cream
1 cup sugar
1 teaspoon corn syrup
1 egg
1 teaspoon vanilla extract
¾ cup apricot preserves,
  slightly heated

**DAY BEFORE PARTY:**

1. Preheat oven to 350°. Grease, then lightly flour 9″ springform pan.

2. In top of double boiler, heat chocolate over hot, not boiling, water until chips melt. In a small mixing bowl, using electric mixer, beat egg yolks slightly, then on low speed, mix in chocolate, melted butter and vanilla extract; set aside. Wash beaters.

3. Beat egg whites and pinch of salt until whites foam, then gradually add the sugar, 1 tablespoon at a time, beating at high speed until whites form stiff peaks.

4. With rubber spatula, mix about ⅓ of egg whites with yolk-chocolate mixture. Sprinkle flour on top. Then gently fold remaining whites into chocolate-flour mixture, until evenly blended. (Don't over-fold.)

5. Pour batter into prepared pan. Bake in center of oven until cake is puffed and a toothpick stuck in the center comes out clean. (Cake will leave sides of pan slightly when done.) This should take about 60 minutes.

6. Remove cake from oven and remove sides of pan. Let cake

cool on rack while preparing glaze. (Before glazing, gently remove bottom of springform pan from cool cake.)

**7. Make Glaze:**

A. In top of double boiler over hot, not boiling, water, melt unsweetened chocolate. Then add cream, sugar and corn syrup. Next, over low, direct heat stir mixture constantly with wooden spoon until chocolate and sugar are completely blended. Raise heat to medium and cook without stirring for about 5 minutes until mixture is gently boiling and a bit of chocolate dropped into a glass of cold water forms a soft ball.

B. In small mixing bowl, beat the egg lightly, then stir 3 or 4 tablespoons of chocolate mixture into it. Pour this into remaining chocolate in saucepan and stir briskly. Cook over low heat, stirring constantly for 2 or 3 minutes until glaze coats spoon heavily. Remove from heat and add vanilla. Cool to room temperature.

**8. Assemble Cake:**

A. With a serrated knife gently cut through center of cake forming 2 even layers. Remove top layer with a spatula.

B. Spread apricot jam on bottom layer; then replace top. Set rack on jelly-roll pan or large dish and holding saucepan with glaze about 2″ away from cake, pour glaze over it evenly. If necessary, smooth glaze with metal spatula. Let cake stand until glaze stops dripping. Then transfer to serving plate and refrigerate.

**AT PARTY TIME:**

1. Remove Sachertorte from refrigerator ½ hour before serving.

# Haselnusstorte
## (Hazelnut Cake)

### The Torte:
6 eggs separated
1 whole egg
⅓ cup bread crumbs
¾ cup sugar
1 cup ground hazelnuts,
  filberts or walnuts
1 teaspoon flour

### The Filling:
1½ cups heavy cream
1 tablespoon sugar
1 teaspoon vanilla extract
⅓ cup ground hazelnuts,
  filberts, or walnuts for
  decoration

**DAY BEFORE PARTY:**

1. Preheat oven to 275°. Butter and flour a 9-inch springform pan.

2. In large bowl, beat 6 egg yolks and whole egg together with electric beater, until mixture is thick and light yellow in color. Gradually beat in ½ cup of sugar, then the nuts and bread crumbs. Beat until mixture is moist and thick.

3. Wash beaters. In another bowl, beat egg whites until foamy, then add ¼ cup of sugar, 1 tablespoon at a time. Beat until whites form stiff peaks. With a rubber spatula, mix about one quarter of whites into hazelnut mixture, then sprinkle flour over it and gently fold in rest of whites. Continue to fold until no trace of whites remains. (*Don't* overfold!)

4. Pour batter into the pan, smooth top with a spatula and bake cake in middle of oven for 40-to-50 minutes, or until torte shrinks away slightly from sides of pan. Remove the side of pan as soon as you take cake from oven; let cake cool, remove bottom of springform pan, then slice cake into two equal layers with a long, serrated knife. Cover cake with plastic wrap; refrigerate until time to assemble.

**TWO HOURS BEFORE SERVING:**
1. With an electric mixer, whip the chilled cream until it begins to thicken. Add sugar and vanilla and continue whipping until cream holds its shape firmly.
2. Assemble the cake by spreading ½ inch of whipped cream on top of first layer; place second layer over it. With spatula, completely cover cake with the rest of the whipped cream.
3. Scatter ⅓ cup of hazelnuts all over cake top and sides to coat completely. Refrigerate until serving time.

## *Vanillekipferl*
## *(Viennese Vanilla Crescents)*

¼ vanilla bean
¾ cup sifted confectioners
   sugar
1 cup walnut meats

2 sticks butter, at room
   temperature
¾ cup granulated sugar
2½ cups sifted all-purpose
   flour

**TWO DAYS BEFORE MAKING COOKIES (ABOUT FOUR DAYS BEFORE PARTY):**
1. Chop vanilla bean. Pound in mortar or pulverize in blender with about 1 tablespoon of confectioners sugar. Then mix with remaining confectioners sugar. Cover and let stand for two days. Reserve while cookies are baked.

**TWO DAYS BEFORE PARTY:**
1. Preheat oven to moderate, 350°.
2. Place walnuts in blender container. Grind until pieces become of paste-like consistency.
3. With wooden spoon or fingers (wear light plastic golves, if

you like), mix walnuts, butter, granulated sugar, and flour until they form a smooth dough. Shape dough, about a teaspoon at a time into small crescents about 1½" across.

4. Bake on ungreased cookie sheet until lightly browned, about 15–18 minutes. Cool 1 minute. While still warm, roll cookies in prepared vanilla sugar.

# *Schaumrolle*
# *(Cream Rolls)*

4 packages of puff pastry
  patty shells (24 shells)
1 beaten egg
granulated sugar

1 pint heavy cream
1 teaspoon almond extract
1 small bar milk chocolate,
  grated

**EARLY ON DAY OF PARTY:**

1. Defrost patty shells for about 1 hour, until dough is soft and workable.

2. Preheat oven to 450°.

3. On floured board, (using 2 shells for each schaumrolle) roll pastry to thickness of ⅛" in a strip about 30" long (for use with cream horn tubes that are 5½" long; for shorter tubes, use shorter strips).

4. Begin at the narrowest end of each tube and wind strip of pastry around tube, slightly overlapping edges. Don't stretch the pastry. Chill for ½ hour.

4. Brush pastry with beaten egg, then coat brushed surface with granulated sugar. Place dough-wrapped tubes 1" apart on waxed paper-lined cookie sheet.

5. Bake at 450° for 10 minutes. Reduce heat to 350° and bake until pastry is golden. Remove tubes from pastry immediately by giving tubes a quick twist to free them. Set aside.

**ONE HOUR BEFORE SERVING:**
1. Add almond extract to cream and whip.
2. Generously fill rolls and garnish with grated chocolate. Refrigerate until serving time.

# *Kaffee*
## *(Coffee)*

If you want to be traditional, try coffee brewed in a tall, narrow-lipped saucepan, called a "Häferl." When serving, vary amount of milk to get anything from a Brauner (dark brown) to a Weisser (hot milk with splash of coffee). Whatever the version selected, it should be topped with a big dollop of whipped cream.

*To Serve 12 (two cups each):*
6 quarts of cold water
24 measures of drip-grind coffee.

**AT SERVING TIME:**
In a large saucepan, cook water and coffee over medium flame until it boils up once. Turn down flame; cover and simmer 5 minutes. Let grounds settle and strain into a coffee pot for serving. Let guests fix their coffee to taste.

# *Schlagobers*
## *(Whipped Cream)*

**ONE OR TWO HOURS BEFORE SERVING:** Whip 2 pints of heavy cream plus 3 teaspoons sugar until stiff. Pile in an attractive bowl; sprinkle with a little nutmeg and serve with coffee.

# Approximate Expenses for an Austrian Jause
## for 12:

| | |
|---|---|
| $ 1.25 | Schinken-Spargelbrot (ham-asparagus canapés) |
| 2.80 | Crevettenbrot (shrimp canapés) |
| 1.15 | Liptauer (cream cheese spread) |
| 4.70 | Russische Eier (Russian eggs) |
| 7.00 | Gumpoldkirschner wine (2 bottles) |
| 2.00 | Sachertorte (chocolate cake) |
| 2.30 | Haselnusstort (hazelnut cake) |
| 1.40 | Vanillekipferl (vanilla crescents) |
| 2.10 | Schaumrolle (cream rolls) |
| 1.60 | Schlagobers (whipped cream) |
| .75 | Kaffee (coffee) |
| $27.05 | Total |

For $2.25 per person you can entertain lavishly at this Austrian Jause for 12.

# Dinners and Suppers for Eight

## Warm Up for a Winter Evening:
## Swiss Supper for 8

There's an annual lull after the Christmas holidays and before Spring when the days seem to drag. Socially, the calendar's fairly dead. Climatically, the weather's pretty depressing. Financially, the budget's in the doldrums because of Christmas gifts and holiday partying.

This is an ideal time to warm up your friends and your spirits (while playing cool with your budget) with a Swiss supper. Schedule it right in the middle of the worst weather—the' end of January or beginning of February.

Switzerland provides an appropriate inspiration for a mid-winter warm-up since the Swiss thrive on cold weather. After Christmas the ski resorts are really swinging; school children even get a special skiing holiday. Après ski, the lodges are lively and, the fondue pots bubble until all hours.

Your own Swiss warm-up can go in any of several directions. You might want to drag out your old ice skates—the ones you haven't used in 20 years—and actually skate for an hour or two. Surely there's a frozen pond nearby just right for amateur efforts. Your husband and friends will probably be just as out of practice as you are, so the entire outing can be an exercise in who falls the least. Take along thermoses of mulled wine and, for the lovers of hardier spirits, warm brandy.

Another idea would be to schedule your Swiss supper for an après-ski party after a day on the slopes. If nobody's brave or brawny enough to skate or ski, put on boots, mufflers et al and go for a walk in the snow, have a snowball fight (girls against boys), or build a snow-man, borrow the kids' sleds and belly-flop down a hill. For once, enjoy the snow instead of complaining about it.

Whatever pre-party sport you choose, the outdoor outing makes coming home to supper something special. Back at the house, informality should be the keynote. If you have a den or family room, schedule the party there. This isn't the time for elegant entertaining with sparkling silver and crystal and pristine linens.

Light a huge fire in the fireplace and throw in some pine boughs for a lovely, wintery scent. It's nice to have guests sprawled on the floor, lounging about on comfortable pillows. (If you lack the TV-watching giant cushions, rustle up some pseudo ones quickly and inexpensively with 2 yards of felt or 4 yards of cordoroy (enough for 4 bed-pillows). The cushions from a chair or sofa that's not in the same room can also be borrowed.

Guests relaxing on pillows and enjoying the fire make for a very cozy setting. But how are they going to deal with the vittles? One solution that works well and achieves just about enough table space at the right height is to set up a card table (don't unfold the legs) propped up on 4 or 5 cinder blocks. You can use a plaid stadium blanket as a tablecloth or make one to match your mock floor pillows.

The food plan for a Swiss supper is fairly representative of the country's cuisine in general. That is, it takes its inspiration from Italy, France, and Germany. Swiss cooking is tri-lingual, just as the country is.

You'll see the influence of all three neighboring countries in this menu. As the Swiss would say "En Guete!" ... or "Bon Appetit." ... or even "Buon Appetito."

# Swiss Supper for 8

### Mulled Wine

### Appetizers

Ramequins De Fromage
(Cheese Tartlets)

Schinkengipfeli
(Ham Croissants)

### Main Course

Fondue Bourguignonne

Béarnaise Sauce    Horseradish Sauce    Caper Sauce

Worcestershire Sauce    Chopped Onions

Spinatsalat
(Spinach Salad)

Züpfe
(Braided Bread)

### Dessert

Apfeltorte Mit Rahm
(Apple Tart with Cream)

Veltliner Wine With Dinner
(or Dôle or Oeil de Perdrix)

Espresso and Brandy
After Dinner

# Mulled Wine

**FOR 18 SERVINGS:**

6 cups burgundy or claret
Peel of 1 orange and
   1 lemon
1 cinnamon stick

1 whole nutmeg, crushed
6 whole cloves
3 teaspoons sugar

**AT PARTY TIME:**

1. Mix all ingredients in a saucepan and simmer gently 5 to 10 minutes. Strain to remove spices and serve hot.

# Ramequins de Fromage
## (Cheese Tartlets)

Switzerland is justifiably famous for its cheese and rich, buttery specialties. In fact, of all the milk produced in the country, only 25% goes into the bottled version for drinking, 39% is made into cheese, and the remaining 36% becomes butter—quite different from the American dairy situation. Here 97.4% of the milk is processed and bottled, while only 1% is used for butter and 1.6% for cheese.

What Americans refer to as "Swiss cheese" is known as Emmenthaler in Switzerland. For Ramequins de Fromage, look for Emmenthaler in a cheese specialty shop or buy imported "Swiss cheese" in your supermarket.

2 boxes pie crust mix or
   enough pastry for 2
   9" pies

3 eggs
1 teaspoon salt
½ teaspoon dry mustard

1½ cups light cream
3 cups grated Emmenthaler
or Swiss cheese

½ teaspoon cayenne pepper

**DAY BEFORE PARTY:**
1. Preheat oven to 400°.
2. Mix pastry; line 2″ tartlet or muffin pans with pie crust. (You should have enough pastry for 24–28 tartlets.) Prick with fork.
3. Bake the shells for about 5–7 minutes until just beginning to color.
4. Beat together cream, cheese, eggs, salt, mustard, and cayenne.
5. Store shells, covered, at room temperature; refrigerate cheese mixture until ready to bake.

**AT PARTY TIME:**
1. Preheat oven to 400°.
2. Spoon cheese mixture into prepared shells, filling each about half full. Bake for about 15 minutes or until golden.

## *Schinkengipfeli*
### *(Ham Croissants)*

2 containers of refrigerator
crescent rolls
sweet butter at room
temperature
½ pound boiled ham, sliced

1 finely chopped onion
2 tablespoons chopped
parsley
1 egg beaten, for glazing

**EARLY ON DAY OF PARTY:**
1. Open one container of crescent rolls; cut each triangle in half.
2. Gently spread light coating of butter on each triangle.
3. Cut ham to fit triangles, place 1 piece of ham neatly on the dough, add some onion and a little parsley and roll up, beginning with smallest side of the triangle. Curve to resemble a croissant. Repeat with second container of rolls. Place on cookie sheet.
4. Brush croissants with egg yolk and refrigerate, covered, until serving time.

**AT PARTY TIME:**
1. Preheat oven to 375°. Bake croissants 10 or 15 minutes or until golden.

# *Fondue Bourguignonne*

While cheese fondue is regarded as the national Swiss dish, and is certainly delightful, after your walk or skating, and certainly after skiing, something a little more substantial might be more welcome. We suggest Fondue Bourguignonne, a dish that has become immensely popular all over the world since World War II.

Fondue Bourguignonne is neither a fondue (no cheese in it) nor is it made with Burgundy wine or inspired by that region. The name is derived from the small pieces of beef, as in *Boeuf à la Bourguignonne* ... and because you dip in order to eat, as in a *fondue.*

| | |
|---|---|
| 5 pounds filet of beef, trimmed of all fat and cut into ¾" cubes | 2 onions |
| | ½ pound butter |
| | 2½ cups peanut oil |
| | 1 cup Worcestershire Sauce |

**EARLY ON DAY OF PARTY:**

1. Cube beef.
2. Make Bearnaise, Horseradish and Caper sauces (see below).
3. Chop onions coarsely; place in small serving dish. Cover with plastic wrap until dinner.

**AT SERVING TIME:**

1. Fondue in Switzerland is cooked in an earthenware pot called a "caquelon." You may use a fondue pan or a chafing dish or electric skillet. (Make sure the cord is well out of everyone's way with an electric fondue pot or skillet.) Heat the butter and oil in the pot on the center of your table. When the oil-butter mixture is bubbling, it's time to start cooking. (During dinner if the oil smokes, cut down the heat or lower the temperature if you're using electrical equipment.)
2. Arrange bowls with chopped onion and Bearnaise, Horseradish, Caper and Worcestershire sauces around fondue pot.
3. Each guest's place-setting should be equipped with a dinner plate and 2 long-pronged forks, one for cooking and one for eating. If you have them, sectioned dishes are perfect for serving fondue. The big section is fine for the meat, a second section holds bread and butter and the third contains the spinach salad. This minimizes the dishes you have to do afterwards, and is an economical way of conserving space on the table which by now is getting a little crowded!
4. Your guests cook their own meat as they like it in the hot oil and butter and then dip the cooked meat in any of the accompanying sauces.
5. There are several traditions about fondue that apply to the bourguignonne variety as well. One decrees that if you drop your bread (in this case, meat) into the cooking pot, you buy the host a bottle of wine; another that may be more fun, rules that if a lady drops her meat into the pot, the men at the table may kiss her; if a man drops his portion into the oil, he may kiss any girl he chooses.

# Béarnaise Sauce

4 tablespoons white wine
2 tablespoons tarragon
    vinegar
4 teaspoons chopped tarragon
4 teaspoons chopped onion
½ teaspoon freshly ground
    black pepper

2 sticks butter
6 egg yolks
4 tablespoons lemon juice
½ teaspoon salt
pinch of cayenne pepper

**EARLY ON DAY OF PARTY (ABOUT THREE HOURS BEFORE SERVING):**
1. In skillet, combine wine, vinegar, tarragon, onions and pepper. Bring to boil and cook rapidly until liquid almost disappears.
2. Heat butter to bubbling in small saucepan. Be careful it doesn't brown.
3. Place egg yolks, lemon juice, salt, and cayenne in blender container. Cover and flick motor on and off at high speed. Remove cover. Turn motor on high and gradually add hot butter.
4. Add herb mixture, cover and blend on high speed four seconds. Set aside, covered.
**AT SERVING TIME:**
1. Reheat béarnaise *slightly* in double boiler over simmering water. *Do Not Boil!*

# Horseradish Sauce

½ cup horseradish, grated
1½ cups sour cream
1 teaspoon sugar

pinch of salt and pepper to
    taste
1½ teaspoons dill

**EARLY ON DAY OF PARTY:**
1. Mix all ingredients together except dill. Chill. At serving time, garnish with dill.

## Caper Sauce

2 tablespoons butter
2 tablespoons flour
1 cup beef bouillon

½ cup heavy cream
2 tablespoons capers
salt and freshly ground black
  pepper to taste

**EARLY ON DAY OF PARTY:**
1. Melt butter in saucepan, add flour and stir with whisk until blended.
2. Bring bouillon to boil and add all at once to butter-flour mixture, stirring vigorously. Cook, stirring constantly, until thick.
3. Add cream, capers and salt and pepper. Set aside, covered.

**AT SERVING TIME:**
1. Reheat sauce gently. *Do not boil!*

## Züpfe
## (Braided Bread)

*Makes Two Loaves:*
1½ cups milk
3 tablespoons sugar
1 tablespoon salt
½ stick of butter
2 packages active dry yeast
½ cup hot water

2 eggs lightly beaten
7 cups unsifted flour
3 tablespoons butter, melted
1 egg yolk, beaten with 1
  tablespoon water

**DAY BEFORE PARTY:**
1. In small saucepan, bring milk to near boil (bubbles form around edge); remove from heat. Add sugar, salt and butter; stir until butter melts. Let cool until lukewarm.
2. Sprinkle yeast over water in large bowl; stir until dissolved. Stir in milk mixture.
3. Add eggs and 3½ cups flour; using a wooden spoon, beat for about 2 minutes until smooth. Gradually add remaining flour, mixing by hand until dough is stiff enough to leave sides of bowl.
4. Turn out on lightly floured board. Knead until dough is smooth and elastic—about 10 minutes.
5. Place in lightly greased bowl; turn dough over to bring up the side that's greased. Cover with dish towel; let rise in a warm place (about 85°) free from drafts, about 1 hour or until double in bulk. (If you like, turn your oven on to low, preheat for 45 minutes or so, turn it off 15 minutes before you want to use it as a rising place for your bread).
6. Return dough to pastry board. Divide in half and divide each half in 3 equal parts. With the palms of the hands, roll each part into a 15-inch long strip. Then braid 3 strips together; pinching the ends together and tucking them underneath neatly. Repeat with other three strips. Place each braid on a greased cookie sheet. Brush with melted butter. Cover with towel. Return braids to your favorite warm place and let rise until double in size—about 1 hour.
7. Preheat oven to 400°. Place oven rack in center of oven.
8. Brush surface of each loaf with egg yolk and water mixture.
9. Bake about 40 minutes or until rich and golden. (Check at 25 minutes and if crust is browning too quickly, cover with aluminum foil). When baked, cool to room temperature before wrapping in foil to store.

**AT PARTY TIME:**
1. Preheat oven to 300°.

2. Reheat foil-wrapped loaves for 10 or 15 minutes until warmed through.

## *Spinatsalat*
## *(Spinach Salad)*

2 pounds very young spinach
2 finely chopped onions
3 tablespoons chopped
   parsley
1 tablespoon chopped chives
½ cup lemon juice

¾ cup olive oil
Salt, pepper to taste
Pinch of sugar
4 hard-boiled eggs, peeled,
   cut in quarters
5 or 6 red radishes, sliced

**EARLY ON DAY OF PARTY:**
1. Wash and dry spinach, patting with clean cloth or paper towels to remove all moisture. Chop finely. Store in refrigerator.
2. Mix onion, parsley and chives together; store in plastic bag and refrigerate.
3. Mix lemon juice, olive oil, salt, pepper, and sugar to taste in a glass jar. Cover, store at room temperature.

**AT SERVING TIME:**
1. Add onion-parsley-chives to chopped spinach. Toss lightly. Shake dressing well. Add to spinach. Toss just to coat leaves. Garnish with quartered eggs and sliced radishes.

## *Apfeltorte Mit Rahm*
## *(Applecake with Cream)*

1½ cups plus 2 table-
   spoons flour

¾ cup sugar
½ teaspoon nutmeg

2 egg yolks

1½ tablespoons sugar

Rind of 1 lemon, grated

¾ cup butter, softened, cut into small cubes

7 or 8 apples, suitable for pie

1 teaspoon lemon juice

1 cup heavy cream

1 egg yolk

¾ cup blanched, slivered almonds

**EARLY ON PARTY DAY:**

1. Sift flour onto sheet of strong plastic (or into bowl). Make a well in center and add egg yolks, sugar, lemon rind, and butter. Mash ingredients together with a fork until somewhat blended.

2. Gather plastic around mixture and knead until dough holds together and forms ball. (If necessary add a teaspoon of ice water to moisten the dough.)

3. Refrigerate for 1 hour (or place in freezer for 30 minutes).

4. Lightly flour a sheet of plastic wrap. Place dough on wrap, place another sheet over it, and roll out to size of 10″ or 11″ glass pie pan (or use metal flan pan). Turn dough into pan; don't worry if it breaks—just patch away. With fingers, flute an attractive edge. Chill shell while you prepare apples.

5. Preheat oven to 350°.

6. Peel, core, slice apples in ¼″ sections. Mix sugar with nutmeg.

7. Arrange apples in a slightly overlapping layer on chilled shell. Sprinkle with half of the sugar-nutmeg mixture and half of lemon juice. Continue to arrange a second layer of apples, until all are used. Sprinkle with remaining sugar-nutmeg and lemon juice.

8. Bake for 25 minutes. In the meantime, beat heavy cream with egg yolk. Sprinkle almonds on apple tart, then pour cream-egg mixture over tart. Cook for another 25 minutes or until fruit is tender and crust is golden.

9. Let cool at room temperature.

**AT SERVING TIME:**
1. Reheat tart for 10 or 15 minutes in a 200° oven. Serve with extra whipped cream for those who defy their waistlines.

## *Expenses for a Swiss Winter Warm-Up for 8:*

| | |
|---|---|
| $ 6.10 | mulled wine |
| 2.75 | Ramequins de Fromage (cheese tartlets) |
| 2.35 | Schinkengipfeli (ham croissants) |
| 15.70 | Fondue Bourguignonne |
| 1.45 | Béarnaise Sauce |
| .65 | Horseradish Sauce |
| .55 | Caper Sauce |
| .40 | Worcestershire sauce |
| .10 | chopped onions |
| 1.15 | Züpfe (braided bread) |
| 1.80 | Spinatsalat (spinach salad) |
| 2.55 | Apfeltorte mit Rahm (applecake with cream) |
| 6.00 | Veltliner Wine (2 bottles) |
| .80 | Espresso |
| 8.00 | Brandy |
| $50.35 | |

For about $6.25 a person you can enjoy a luxurious and authentic Swiss warm-up for 8 guests.

# The Elegant Touch: French Dinner
# À La Provençale for 8

Shortly after mastering hamburgers, some of us who cook (out of need or pleasure, or both) feel the urge to conquer haute cuisine ... and we spend the next twenty or thirty years in the pursuit thereof. (Interspersed with cooking thousands of hamburgers, gallons of spaghetti sauce, hundreds of steaks and the various specialty dishes served to appreciative and demanding families and, hopefully, appreciative guests.)

Somewhere along the road to cuisine perfection, however, I opted for some side trips on paths less esoteric. I respect, admire, and love to eat the concoctions of Escoffier, Brilla-Savarin and friends ... I collect all the descriptions and recipes of France's four-star restaurants ... I badger my husband all year long to take me to New York's famous bastions of haute cuisine (where he will invariably order a steak). But when it comes to entertaining, give me something a little less delicate to work with. True, classically elegant, French food doesn't wait well, and by now you know I like to play hostess, not chef when giving a party.

With the emphasis then on the total entertaining picture (not simply the ability to turn out a superb sauce and rush it immediately to the table), this French-accented chapter concentrates on the Provençale district; the menu might be described as "country" rather than "elegant".... although the menu is not exactly a French version of hot dogs and French fries.

The selections are zesty and straightforward—no subtle tastes that could go undetected by those of us with less refined palates. And the entire feast is an excellent example of blessed, do-ahead cuisine. All you'll have to do is take things out of the oven and toss the salad: the dressing's already prepared.

Since the atmosphere is informal, try to achieve a true "provincial" feeling with your table-setting. If you're planning on flowers for a centerpiece, buy a big bunch of casual blooms and arrange them informally yourself. Daisies, mums, tulips and the like, according to what's in season, are more in keeping with the tone of the dinner than rich roses in a stiff arrangement, or another floristy-looking bouquet.

If your table is large enough, include both a salad plate and bread and butter dish for each guest; if the result, with dinner for eight, will seem crowded, skip the bread-and-butter setting and pre-butter the bread before heating it in the oven.

It's nice to serve cocktails that complement the dinner theme, but this can get a little sticky because many people have their tried and true favorites (which they prefer at *any* cocktail hour), but try anyway. In any case, keep the cocktail hour short. This is a rich dinner and a drink should really be an apéritif —something to pick up the appetite, not kill it. Some unusual "cocktails" that work well with this dinner include Lillet, slightly orange-ish in flavor, nice when served on the rocks with a bit of orange or lemon peel and a splash of soda; Byrrh (pronounce it "beer"), served cold with a lemon twist; dry vermouth on its own—an ideal apéritif when served on the rocks or chilled in a cocktail glass, Creme de Cassis, mixed with club soda and dry vermouth becomes a Vermouth Cassis, or add a few drops of Cassis to a glass of champagne and you'll have a champagne cocktail. (I think this last is a bit too grand for our provençale evening.)

The menu that follows is appropriate for any time of the year. In fact, Vichyssoise, eminently suitable for summer is featured as the potage. Now, I know that Vichyssoise sounds très elegante, especially when it's pronounced properly (Vichy-swazze, *not* Vichy-swah). But when you think about it, this lovely soup—I must say it's my favorite—is really peasant fare, the main ingredients being potatoes and leeks! If you decide to serve your provençale dinner in the dead of winter, serve the Vichyssoise *hot* instead of *cold* and call it "Potage Parmentier."

Keep the atmosphere lightly French with songs by Gallic notables such as Maurice Chevalier, Edith Piaf, and other bistro-type singers. (Three exceptional recordings are "Young Chevalier," Capitol T-10360, "The Best of Edith Piaf," Capitol DT 2616 and "The Little Sparrow," Phillips, PCC 208).

Now, do all your work ahead of time, give a final touch to your appealing table setting . . . and prepare to enjoy a delicious meal that runs smoothly from pâté to tarte.

# French Dinner À La Provençale for 8

Apéritifs: Lillet, Byrrh, Dry Vermouth, etc.

## Les Hors D'Oeuvres

Pâté Provençale              Camembert En Croute
(Pâté with Toast Triangles)   (Camembert Cheese in Pastry)
Crudités (Raw Vegetables with Sauce)

## Le Potage
Vichyssoise

## L'Entree

Boeuf en Daube à la Provençale
(Beef Stew with Vegetables)
Salade Forestière              French Bread/Sweet Butter

## L'Entremet
Tarte Aux Abricots (Apricot Tart)

Demi-Tasse

Brandy

Wine: a full-bodied burgundy, Chateauneuf-du-Pape
or Côtes-du-Rhone with dinner

# Pâté Provençale

2 pounds coarsely chopped
   lean pork
2 pounds finely chopped veal
1 pound pork liver, ground
4 garlic cloves, minced
3 eggs

½ cup cognac
1 tablespoon basil
1 teaspoon tarragon
1 tablespoon salt
freshly ground black pepper
   to taste
½ pound bacon or enough to
   line casserole

**DAY BEFORE PARTY:**
1. Combine all ingredients except bacon. Taste a bit to test for seasoning.
2. Line a 2½ quart soufflle dish or straight-sided terrine or other deep baking dish with bacon. Fill with mixture and shape neatly on top. Place a few additional strips of bacon on top and bake at 300° for 2½ hours to 3 hours. (Cover pâté with aluminum foil for the first hour.) When pâté is done it will leave the sides of the casserole.
3. Remove from oven and cool. After 30 minutes, place a heavy dish on top. Refrigerate overnight.

**AT SERVING TIME:**
1. Remove pâté from refrigerator about 1 hour before serving.
2. Serve in casserole with toast triangles.

# Camembert En Croute

½ cup sifted all-purpose flour
¼ teaspoon salt
¼ cup cream cheese
   (¼ of an 8-ounce package)

1 7 or 8 ounce imported
   camembert, about 4″ in
   diameter

½ stick of butter

1 egg yolk, slightly beaten
with 2 teaspoons water

**DAY BEFORE PARTY:**
1. Make pastry. Sift flour with salt into a small bowl. With blender or two forks, cut in cream cheese and butter until mixture looks like coarse corn meal. Shape pastry into ball; wrap in plastic wrap and refrigerate.

**EARLY ON DAY OF PARTY:**
1. On lightly floured board, roll out dough to ⅛" thickness. Cut out a 7" to 8" circle using pastry wheel or knife. Place on cookie sheet. Center camembert cheese on pastry. Bring pastry up around side of cheese and ¾" over top of cheese. Press dough smooth.
2. Re-roll trimmings. Cut a circle to fit top of cheese.
3. Brush some of the egg yolk on rim of pastry on top of cheese. Place pastry circle on top, crimping slightly to seal. With trimmings, cut out several leaves, and a long strip of pastry. Roll strip of pastry in rosebud fashion and place with leaves in center of pastry. Brush with rest of egg mixture. Refrigerate.

**AT PARTY TIME:**
1. Preheat oven to 450°. Bake Camembert en Croute about 15–20 minutes until golden brown. Cool for about 20 minutes before serving. Cut in wedges; use small forks and dishes.

# Crudités

*Sauce:*

1 cup mayonnaise
1 tablespoon Dijon mustard

*Vegetables:*

cherry tomatoes
scallions

a dash of tabasco
4 tablespoons chopped
  parsley

celery sticks
raw mushroom caps
carrot sticks
cucumber fingers
green pepper strips
radishes

**EARLY ON DAY OF PARTY:**
1. Mix together ingredients for sauce.
2. Wash vegetables. Slice celery, carrots, cucumbers and green pepper.

**AT SERVING TIME:**
1. Arrange vegetables attractively on serving tray. Place sauce in center for dipping.

## Vichyssoise

5 large potatoes, peeled and
  sliced very thin
4 leeks, white part only,
  thinly chopped
1 medium-sized onion,
  peeled and minced
1 stick of butter
2 13¾-ounce cans chicken
  broth, undiluted

1 tablespoon fresh lemon
  juice
freshly ground white
  pepper to taste
1½ cups milk
2 cups light cream
½ cup heavy cream
chopped chives for garnish

**DAY BEFORE PARTY:**
1. Cook potatoes, leeks, and onion in butter with salt to taste over very low flame until vegetables begin to look golden.

2. Add chicken broth, lemon juice and pepper; simmer slowly about 1 hour. Put into blender to purée. Then return to saucepan.
3. Add milk and light cream; slowly bring to simmer; remove from heat; put through blender once more.
4. Cool to room temperature. Stir in heavy cream. Taste to correct seasonings. Cover, refrigerate overnight.

**AT SERVING TIME:**
1. One hour before serving, rinse out soup tureens, and while still wet, place in freezer.
2. At serving time, pour vichyssoise into bowls, sprinkle with chopped chives; pass around pepper mill. (Note: to serve hot, eliminate step 1; re-heat soup gently, serve as in step 2.)

## Boeuf En Daube à La Provençale

*Marinade:*

⅓ cup olive oil
3 onions, sliced
1 stalk celery, cut in chunks
1 carrot, cut in chunks
3 cloves garlic, minced
2 teaspoons salt

½ teaspoon rosemary
½ teaspoon thyme
1 teaspoon of black
  peppercorns
2 cups dry white wine
  (vermouth is fine)

*Daube:*

4 pounds top round, cut in
  1½″ cubes
¼ pound salt pork
16 small white onions, peeled
¾ cup dry white wine
3 cups beef stock or bouillon
1 teaspoon salt

8 carrots, peeled and cut in
  half
1 cup pitted green olives
  drained
1 cup pitted black olives
  drained
1 box cherry tomatoes, peeled

| ½ teaspoon rosemary | Freshly ground black pepper |
| 2 cloves garlic, crushed | to taste |

## TWO DAYS BEFORE PARTY:
### MAKE MARINADE:
1. Heat olive oil in saucepan. Add onions, celery, carrots and garlic. Sauté until onion is tender. Add remaining marinade ingredients and simmer 15 minutes. Stir occasionally. Place marinade in bowl and cool. Add beef cubes, cover and refrigerate overnight. Stir occasionally.

## DAY BEFORE PARTY:
1. Remove beef from marinade. Pat meat dry with paper towels. Strain marinade and set aside (you'll have about 1 cup liquid). Discard vegetables from marinade.
2. Blanch salt pork in boiling water for 8–10 minutes. Remove from water and cut into ½" cubes. Brown salt pork in large skillet. Brown beef cubes in same skillet. When brown on all sides, transfer to oven-proof casserole. Next, brown onions in the fat and set aside.
3. Preheat oven to 350°. Pour drained marinade into casserole with meat; add wine and just enough beef bouillon to cover. Add salt, rosemary and garlic; cover, cook in oven about 1¼ hours.
4. Add reserved onions and carrots and cook 45 minutes longer, until vegetables and meat are tender. Remove from oven; let cool to room temperature. Refrigerate, covered, overnight.

## AT PARTY TIME:
1. Remove from refrigerator about one hour before serving. Skim fat from surface.
2. Preheat oven to 300°. Heat daube for about 20 minutes until warmed through. Five minutes before serving, rinse olives and add to stew. Add the peeled tomatoes, plus pepper. Test for seasoning before serving.
Note: To peel tomatoes: Drop into boiling water for a few sec-

onds. (not more than 10). Then pour into collander and slip skins off; they should be quite easy to peel.

## Salade Forestière

| | |
|---|---|
| 1 pound mushrooms | salt and pepper to taste |
| ½ cup lemon juice | 6 cups mixed salad greens |
| ½ cup olive oil | (Boston lettuce and |
| ¼ cup corn oil | chicory, for example) |

**EARLY ON DAY OF PARTY:**
1. Trim stems of mushrooms, wash and dry carefully. Slice through caps and stems into very thin pieces.
2. Combine lemon juice, olive and corn oil, salt and pepper in a glass jar. Shake well and pour over mushrooms. Refrigerate.
3. Prepare salad greens; refrigerate.

**AT SERVING TIME:**
1. Add mushrooms and dressing to greens. Toss gently. Serve on individual salad plates.

## Tarte Aux Abricots

**DAY BEFORE PARTY:**
*MAKE SWEET PASTRY:*

| | |
|---|---|
| 2 cups sifted all purpose flour | 2 sticks sweet butter, |
| 2 egg yolks | softened |
| 2 tablespoons sugar | Rind of 1 lemon, grated |
| Pinch of salt | ice water |

1. Sift flour onto sheet of strong plastic. Make a well in center and add remaining ingredients except ice water.
2. Mix the center ingredients with pastry blender until well blended. Fold paper around in ball form and quickly work ingredients together. Add a small amount of ice water if necessary to gather dough into ball.
3. Wrap dough and chill in freezer 1 hour.
4. On lightly floured board, cover top surface of dough with plastic wrap and roll until about 8″ in diameter. Flip pastry over and keep rolling until it's large enough to fit a 12″ flan pan with at least 2″ over hang around.
5. Turn pastry into pan, finish off edges decoratively, prick with a fork all over, and bake in preheated 450° oven for 10 minutes. (If pastry comes apart while you're trying to get it into pan, don't worry, simply patch it—it won't show.) After shell is cooked, cool, then cover with plastic wrap. Refrigerate overnight.

**EARLY ON DAY OF PARTY:**
*MAKE CRÈME PÂTISSIÈRE* (custard filling).

## Crème Pâtissière:

| | |
|---|---|
| 2 cups milk | ½ teaspoon cornstarch |
| ½ teaspoon vanilla extract | ½ cup sugar |
| ½ cup less 1 tablespoon flour | 4 egg yolks |

1. Heat milk with vanilla.
2. Combine flour and cornstarch and add to sugar and egg yolks in a saucepan. Beat thoroughly.
3. Add a little hot milk to egg mixture and stir well.
4. Over low heat, gradually combine the two mixtures, stirring constantly until thick. *Don't* let mixture boil. Cool to room temperature.

**ONE HOUR BEFORE SERVING:**
*ASSEMBLE TART:*

½ cup apricot preserves
¼ cup slivered almonds
2 tablespoons sugar
1 large can of apricots, halved
   and pitted; or 8–10 fresh
   apricots, peeled, halved
   and pitted

1. Boil apricot preserves and sugar together in a small saucepan for 2 or 3 minutes until just thick enough to coat back of spoon lightly. Use half of the glaze to coat inside of pastry shell. Let set for 5 minutes.
2. Next, spread a ½″ to ¾″ layer of pastry cream in the bottom of the shell.
3. Arrange drained apricot halves in attractive fashion. Sprinkle with slivered almonds and coat with remainder of apricot glaze.

## Expenses for a French Dinner À La Provençale for 8:

| | |
|---|---|
| $ 5.00 | Aperitifs (Lillet, Byrrh, Dry Vermouth, etc.) |
| 9.55 | Pâté Provençale |
| 1.30 | Camembert en Croute |
| 2.10 | Crudités |
| 2.50 | Vichyssoise |
| 12.30 | Boeuf en Daube à la Provençale |
| 1.80 | Salade Forestière |
| .40 | French bread |
| .20 | Sweet butter |
| 2.35 | Tarte aux Abricots |
| .75 | Demi-Tasse |
| 3.00 | Brandy |
| 6.00 | Chateauneuf-du-Pape or other burgundy (2 bottles) |

$47.25

You can serve 8 guests this delicious French dinner for less than $6.00 a person—and this includes brandies and wines!

# Take a Roman Holiday with an Italian Dinner for 8

'Twas said, "All roads lead to Rome," and some of the proof is still around if you travel through England, France, Switzerland, Greece, the near East, and a good many other exotic, locales. Gastronomically speaking, that statement also holds true since one can trace much of the inspiration for modern European (and therefore, in large measure, American cooking) to what either originated with or was borrowed by those enterprising Italians, especially during the time of the Roman empire and later, during the Renaissance.

Mind you, I said originated *or* borrowed. I wouldn't dare claim sole creativity for the Italians lest I be lynched by Greeks, Turks, Arabs, Moors, Chinese and others whose cooking the Italians adapted to their own taste.

Legend has it that Marco Polo brought the noodle back from China with him in the fourteenth century, but earlier books (specifically one dated around 1290) indicate that Italians were already enjoying their pasta at least a decade before the great trip to China. Marco Polo did, however, import spices and herbs from the mysterious east which even today make Italian cuisine so zesty and "simpatico."

Italians were the first to make a delicacy out of ice cream, but they did *not* invent it. True ice cream as we know it today was an Italian product "inherited" from the Arabs during one of their invasions in the 9th century. To be fair, the Arabs had learned the technique from the Chinese!

Many people practically identify Italy with tomatoes, but Rome never knew a tomato until Cortez brought them back from Mexico. The French called tomatoes "pommes d'amour" (love apples), and the Italians call them "pomodoro" (golden apples) because the first ones ever seen in Europe were yellow, not red. We must, though, credit the green-thumbed inhabitants of the boot for cultivating, crossbreeding, and engaging in all those other mysterious horticultural adventures which finally produced the lovely red, ripe tomato much as we know it today. (Obviously, I don't mean those sun-lamped, super-market disappointments).

The Romans did enjoy cottage cheese and because of their passion for what is now known as "ricotta" invented cheesecake, 2,000 years ago. They were also the first to have professional bakers in 170 A.D. This coincided with the refinement of grain to a real, flour-like product called "farina." What wasn't used to bake bread was used to powder the noses of upper-class ladies who frequented the Forum.

In those dear, dead, decadent days the wealthy thought cabbage was a delicacy for the very elite, which promised great restorative powers. Conversely, the poor were forced to enjoy nettles, cardoons, and other greens which today, ironically, are considered special.

The Renaissance in Italy brought about the rebirth—in fact, the true development—of Italian cooking. One of the most enduring inventions of the Italian Renaissance was the *fork*.

Catherine de Medici then let her countrymen down. As part of her dowry when she left Italy to marry Henry II of France, she took along not only hundreds of recipes, but also a full staff of chefs to teach Italian cooking secrets to the "backward" French. And there lies a tale. Haute cuisine, which today is generally identified as a French contribution, is actually the product of the Italians, and through the Italians, so many, many other peoples who lent their methods and foods and customs.

However, Italians, while dealt a rather hard blow by Signora de Medici, came back culinarily speaking and by the 18th century were undauntedly on their way to greater cookery triumphs.

Italy, while not a large country in terms of area, is gigantic in terms of diversity of food preparation. Every region has its own specialties and each is quite chauvinistic about preparing them. Here at home, a hot dog in New York is pretty much like a hot dog in Des Moines, or Albuquerque, or downtown Burbank. But in Italy, there's nothing like Neapolitan pizza . . . really nothing like it, and pizza in Bologna is liable to be garnished with spinach, while pizza in Piedmont might (if you bought it in an expensive restaurant) be topped off with a truffle. "Trippa alla Fiorentina" is tripe stewed in chicken broth with herbs and vegetables; "Busecca" (from Lombardy) is tripe that insists on quite a different set of vegetables; "Trippa alla Siciliana" languishes in a tomato sauce, while "Guagghiarid" is the Neapolitan version of tripe grandly stuffed with lamb's liver, salami, cheese, parsley, and eggs!

One thing that unites Italians, however, aside from their interest in music and a generally cavalier outlook on life, is the seriousness with which they take their pasta. There are more than 50 versions of pasta, ranging from the smallest "conchigliette" and "acini de pepe" for soup to the grand "lasagne" and "cannelloni" for baking or stuffing. In between are the so-called "cut macaroni," including "mostaccioli" and "grosso rigato."

For the purist, pasta is *spaghetti* with its many variations, all skinny and delicate. I personally like "fat" pasta (give me a good dish of ziti with sauce and meatballs any day). My very-Scottish husband insists on spaghettini #9 or #10 and was seconded in his choice by my grandmother who came to America almost 80 years ago. She told him: "Cut macaroni is for the children; the men always have spaghetti!"

In any case, Italians have glorified pasta in general to the point where in Potedassio, (in Liguria) there is a spaghetti museum with ancient machines for making pasta. They even have papal bulls from the 13th century, setting forth regulations about how pasta should be made!

Whether you opt for mostaccioli, spaghetti, polenta, or those nice little anguille-eels, there's something for everybody in Italian cuisine. I think to do justice to the glory that was Rome (if you want to be that formal about it) or just take a quick dip into the total pool of Italian food, it would be fun to go on a Roman holiday and sample a little bit from several regions.

But to have an entertaining Italian Night, you can't simply rely on food. An Italian adage insists that a good evening should include "buon'amici, buon canzone, buon prazo, e buon vino." Good friends, good songs, good dinner, and good wine.

The good friends are up to you. As for the good songs, they can range all the way from Grand Opera to homespun regional ballads. Opera may be a little hard to talk by, or romanticize over, however (and if you're going to have an Italian evening, you might as well be romantic), so try some Italian popular songs by such performers as Liciano Virgili ("Addio Signora," "Bambina," "Innamorata") or Sergio Bruni ("My Naples," "Te Voglia Bene").

About the buon pranzo. We'll borrow from the Chinese and take one from column A, one from column B. As you'll see in the menu below, we've tried to feature some regional specialties from the leading areas of Italy.

And now about the buon vino. Italian wine may not be as aristocratic as French wine, but it does have its moments. For your Roman holiday, utilize a little vermouth from Piedmont and campari from Lombardy; for dinner, some valpolicella (Verona) or verdicchio (Marches, central Italy), and to wind it all up, while your guests sit back and enjoy the enchanting ballads, sip either strega or galliano, from Benevento (region of Naples) and Solaro (Tuscany).

Before the menu. They say the Greeks had a word for it . . . but so do the Italians. Perhaps "See Naples and Die" . . . or "Vini, Vidi, Vici" don't mean too much to you. But who can forget such tantalizing ideas as "La Dolce Vita" . . . "Dolce Far Niente" (the sweet-do-nothing), or, and this is much grander, "L'arte de godere"—the art of enjoying life. Enjoy life with this dinner party, sit back and for a while pretend that "la vita" is really "dolce." Buon'appetit!

# Italian Dinner for 8

## Apperitivi

Americanos                    Perfect Martinis

## Antipasti

Bagna Cauda (Piedmont)         Vongole Ripiene (Genoa)
(Raw Vegetables with hot sauce)      (Stuffed Clams)

## Pasta

Manicotti Al Forno (Sicily)
(Baked Manicotti)

## Carne E Salata (Meat and Salad)

Scaloppini Di Vitelli Al Marsala (Milan)
(Veal Scallopini with Marsala Wine)

Insalata Di Carciofi (Lombardy)          Pane E Burro
(Artichoke Salad)                  (Bread and Butter)

## Dolci (Desserts)

Biscuit Tortoni (Naples)          Biscotti Al Mandorle (Rome)
(Cream Pudding)                (Almond Cookies)

Espresso                    Galliano or Strega

Verdicchio or Valpolicella with Dinner

# *Americanos*

A crucial part of this apèritif is the sweet vermouth, produced in the Piedmont region. The word vermouth comes from the German "wermut," for wormwood, also used in making absinthe. During the middle ages, it was believed that vermouth had medicinal powers. Today, the claims for those powers have abated somewhat, but vermouth is still said to aid digestion and supposed to be effective in treating hangovers.

### *For Eight Americanos:*

4 cups sweet vermouth
1½ cups Campari bitters'
Strips of orange peel

Club soda
Ice cubes
8-ounce wine glasses

### EARLY ON DAY OF PARTY:
1. Mix sweet vermouth and Campari in a glass jar. Refrigerate.

### AT SERVING TIME:
1. Fill glasses about half-full with vermouth and Campari mixture. Rub orange peel over each glass to release oil and drop peel into glass. Add several ice cubes, fill with club soda and stir.

# *Perfect Martinis*

Unlike a dry martini, the perfect variety includes both sweet and dry vermouth. As a change from the regular cocktail standby, try the Perfect version for your Italian dinner:

**For Eight Perfect Martinis:**

½ cup sweet vermouth
½ cup dry vermouth

1½ cups gin
Strips of lemon peel
Cocktail glasses

**EARLY ON DAY OF PARTY:**
1. Mix both vermouths and gin in a glass jar. Refrigerate.

**AT SERVING TIME:**
1. Fill cocktail glasses. Twist lemon peel over each glass to release oil, then drop peel into cocktail.

# Bagna Cauda
## (Raw Vegetables with Hot Sauce)

Bagna Caude, a Piemontese specialty, literally means a hot bath for the raw vegetables and grissini that accompany it. This Italian version of the French crudités is often regarded as a complete meal in Piedmont, especially when paired with wine, bread and cheese.

*Sauce:* mix together

1 quart olive oil
8 garlic cloves, finely cut
14–15 anchovy fillets,
    finely chopped
salt and freshly ground black
    pepper to taste
1 teaspoon rosemary
1 teaspoon oregano

*Vegetables:*

Cherry tomatoes
Green pepper sticks
Carrot sticks
Cucumber fingers
Cauliflowerets
Radishes
Raw mushroom caps
Scallions
Grissini (breadsticks)

**EARLY ON DAY OF PARTY:**
1. Mix ingredients for sauce together; set aside. Prepare vegetables. Refrigerate.

**AT SERVING TIME:**
Heat sauce; then keep it hot in a fondue pot or chafing dish. Arrange vegetables attractively. (To enjoy Bagna Cauda, vegetables and grissini are dipped in the hot sauce).

# *Vongole Ripiene*
## *(Stuffed Clams)*

32 little neck clams
1 cup seasoned Italian
 breadcrumbs
1 teaspoon oregano
2 tablespoons grated
 Parmesan cheese
5 tablespoons olive oil

½ cup dry vermouth or other
 dry white wine
1 teaspoon salt
freshly ground black pepper
½ cup finely chopped Italian
 parsley for garnish

**EARLY ON DAY OF PARTY:**
1. Open clams, discard top shell, loosen clams from shell and reserve liquid.
2. Using scissors, mince clams. Combine breadcrumbs, oregano, cheese, olive oil, vermouth, salt and pepper; mix lightly and add the clams.
3. Fill each shell with a good dollop of stuffing. Strain the reserved clam juice and pour a little on each shell.
4. Place clams on baking sheets. Cover with plastic wrap and store in refrigerator.

**AT SERVING TIME:**
1. Remove stuffed clams from refrigerator about an hour before serving.
2. Preheat oven to 400°.
3. Bake clams for 7–10 minutes or until crumbs are golden brown. If your oven is slow, broil them for the last few minutes.
4. Serve hot, garnished with parsley.

# *Manicotti Al Forno*

**Grandma's Sauce:**
1 35-ounce can Italian tomatoes
1 6-ounce can tomato paste
1 teaspoon salt
1 teaspoon sugar
1 teaspoon sweet basil
½ teaspoon pepper
2 tablespoons corn oil
½ pound of chuck
½ pound of pork butt
1 small onion, coarsely chopped
2 cloves of garlic, minced

**Shells:**
1 cup flour
1 cup water
4 eggs
½ teaspoon salt
1 teaspoon butter

**Filling:**
2 pounds ricotta cheese
1 pound mozzarella, diced
1 egg, beaten
⅓ cup grated Parmesan cheese
1 teaspoon salt
¼ teaspoon pepper

**DAY BEFORE PARTY:**
*MAKE THE SAUCE:*
1. Put the tomatoes and their liquid through the blender, briefly. Place purée in medium-sized saucepan and mix in paste. Add salt, sugar, basil and pepper. Fill the 35-ounce tomato can and the paste can with water; add to saucepan. (This utilizes any tomato left in the cans—plus it's the right amount of water to

use!) Cook over medium heat.

2. Meanwhile, heat oil in a skillet and add beef and pork. Brown slowly on all sides (about 10 minutes). Remove meat and in the same skillet, sauté onion and garlic sntil lightly browned. Add 2 tablespoons of water to the frying pan to get all the bits of onion, garlic end brown bits of meat. Empty contents into saucepan with tomato mixture and meat.

3. Cook slowly for 1½ to 2 more hours, stirring occasionally. Taste for seasoning and add more salt if necessary. Cool for about half an hour and refrigerate.

### MAKE MANICOTTI SHELLS:

1. In medium bowl combine the flour, water, eggs, and salt. Beat with an electric mixer until smooth.

2. Melt butter in a 5-inch skillet. The pan should be hot enough so that a drop of water immediately disappears. Using a plastic measuring spoon from a container of coffee (2 tablespoons) as a measure, fill with batter and pour into frying pan, tilting pan quickly to spread batter evenly over bottom of pan. Cook just until bubbles form on the top; then quickly, with a small spatula, turn and cook a few more seconds, only until bottom is *very* lightly browned. Remove from pan; cool on wire rack. Continue cooking batter, until all is used; you'll have 18–20 shells. Set aside.

### MAKE FILLING:

1. Combine ricotta, mozzarella, egg, Parmesan cheese, salt and pepper, blending well with a wooden spoon.

### ASSEMBLE MANICOTTI:

1. Place about ¼ cup of filling in the center of each shell; bring one side of the shell toward the center; overlap with the other side so that you have an elongated looking cigar shape.

2. Place seam side down on a baking sheet for storage. Cover and refrigerate overnight.

**AT SERVING TIME:**
1. Preheat oven to 300°.
2. Heat sauce gently for half an hour before serving.
3. 15 minutes before serving, spoon about ½ cup of sauce into each of 2 attractive baking dishes you can present at the table. Place the manicotti, seam side down, in single layers in each dish. Cover generously with sauce, reserving at least 2 cups to serve separately in a gravy boat during dinner.
4. Sprinkle manicotti with a little grated Parmesan cheese and bake, uncovered for 15 minutes or until bubbling.

# *Scaloppini Di Vitello Al Marsala*
## *(Veal Scallopini with Marsala Wine)*

2 pounds veal cutlets, cut into very thin slices, about 4" × 4"
1 cup flour seasoned with 1 teaspoon salt and freshly ground black pepper
4 tablespoons butter
4 tablespoons olive oil

5 or 6 chopped shallots or small white onions, chopped
1 pound fresh, sliced mushrooms
2 tablespoons chopped Italian parsley
½ teaspoon tarragon
1 cup Marsala wine

**TWO OR THREE HOURS BEFORE PARTY:**
1. Dredge veal in seasoned flour.
2. Heat butter and oil in skillet and sauté veal until browned on both sides. Place veal in oven-proof casserole you can serve in.
3. When all veal slices are browned, add chopped shallots or onions to pan; sauté for 2 minutes.
4. Add mushrooms; sauté 2 minutes more.

5. Stir in chopped parsley, tarragon, and half the Marsala wine. Allow to cook down for a minute or two. Add the remaining Marsala, cook for another few seconds before you pour the sauce over the veal.
6. Cover and let stand at room temperature.

**AT SERVING TIME:**
1. Reheat veal in 200° oven for 10 or 15 minutes or until heated through.

# *Insalata Di Carciofi*
## *(Artichoke Salad)*

⅓ cup olive oil
⅓ cup salad or vegetable oil
¼ cup wine vinegar
1 teaspoon salt

freshly ground black pepper
2 packages thawed frozen
    artichoke hearts
2 heads romaine lettuce,
    torn for salad

**DAY BEFORE PARTY:**
1. Mix oils, vinegar, salt and pepper in a large glass jar until well blended. Add artichoke hearts and marinate overnight.

**AT SERVING TIME:**
1. In large bowl, add romaine and artichoke hearts, plus the dressing. Toss gently; taste for seasoning.

# Biscuit Tortoni
## (Cream Pudding)

2 cups milk
4 eggs, separated
1½ cups sugar
2 packages gelatin
2 tablespoons milk at room
   temperature

1 tablespoon brandy
Salt
4 tablespoons sugar
1 pint heavy cream, whipped
1 square of unsweetened
   chocolate, grated

**DAY BEFORE PARTY:**
1. Scald milk in a saucepan.
2. In the top of a double boiler, beat egg yolks well; then add scalded milk and sugar. Dissolve gelatin in 2 tablespoons milk and stir into egg yolk mixture. Cook over boiling water, stirring constantly, until mixture comes to a boil and gelatin is completely dissolved. Stir in brandy and pinch of salt. Set aside to cool.
3. When egg yolk mixture is nearly cooled to room temperature, beat egg whites until stiff, gradually adding 4 tablespoons of sugar.
4. Fold egg whites into egg yolk mixture; gently fold in whipped cream.
5. Turn into serving dishes (champagne glasses work fine); decorate with grated chocolate. Refrigerate overnight.

# Biscotti Al Mandorle
## (Almond Cookies)

½ pound almonds
1 cup butter (2 sticks)

2 cups flour
yolk of 1 egg

1 cup sugar
2 whole eggs

grated rind of 1 lemon

**TWO OR THREE DAYS BEFORE PARTY:**
1. Grate almonds in blender or with hand grater. (Reserve ¼ cup almonds for garnish.)
2. Cream butter, add ¾ cup sugar, eggs, flour and almonds. Chill.
3. Roll thin and cut in strips or squares.
4. Brush with egg yolk, sprinkle with reserved nuts and remaining ¼ cup sugar and bake in a 350° oven for 10 or 12 minutes until nicely brown.

# Caffé Espresso

If you don't happen to have a nifty little Italian espresso-maker (and I don't happen to), you can obtain pretty praiseworthy results with a standard coffee pot.

*For 20 Demitasse Cups:*
10 cups cold water          20 tablespoons Italian roast coffee

Brew as you would regular coffee. Don't perk more than 5 or 6 minutes. Serve with small slivers of lemon.

## Expenses for a Roman Holiday
## Dinner Party for 8:

$ 4.75     Americanos

| | |
|---|---|
| 2.80 | Perfect Martinis |
| 4.40 | Bagna Cauda (raw vegetables) |
| 5.25 | Vongole Ripiene (stuffed clams) |
| 4.45 | Manicotti al Forno (baked manicotti) |
| 9.90 | Scaloppini di Vitelli (veal scallopini) |
| 2.25 | Insalata di Carciofi (artichoke salad) |
| 1.00 | Pane e Burro (bread and butter) |
| 1.00 | Tortoni (cream pudding) |
| 1.40 | Biscotti al Mandorle (almond cookies) |
| .75 | Espresso |
| 5.00 | Galliano or Strega (half a bottle) |
| 7.00 | Verdicchio or Valpolicella (2 bottles) |
| $50.95 | |

$6.25 per person is the approximate cost for this Roman Holiday. Remember, it does include cocktails, wine and brandy as well as food.

# Salute Ireland at a Gala
# St. Patrick's Day Dinner Party for 8

Every March 17 is a great day for the Irish . . . and anyone else touched by the special magic of St. Patrick's Day celebrations.

In Ireland, of course, March 17th is a national holiday, characterized by wearin' of the green (by everybody!), religious services, champion sports matches, traditional dances and singing, holiday fare and quite a bit of liquid imbibing.

In America, the most notable event is the St. Patrick's Day Parade held every year on New York's Fifth Avenue ever since 1784. You might say that Ireland and America have quite a bit in common in commemorating St. Patrick: it's definitely a fine day, "Lá breá (pronounce it law braw) . . . and most certainly a "wet" day, "Lá fliuch" (say law flukh).

To be realistic, I think the Irish have been rather unfairly portrayed as a nation of heavy drinkers. Yes, they do like their stout and beer, but of the Irish Republic's population of 3,000,000, 16% are teetotalers who wear temperance badges with pride. By the same token, the per capita drinking of Ireland is well below that of European countries and the English, Germans, Australians, and Americans all drink more beer per person.

Now that we've cleared that up, we can safely establish that, despite statistics, it wouldn't be St. Patrick's Day without taking a wee drop (or two) to celebrate. In Ireland, that drop will usually be pints of stout or shots of Irish Whiskey.

The most popular stout is Guinness's Dublin (and no wonder, since Guinness is the largest employer in Ireland. As observed in most parts of the world, you don't bite the hand that feeds you!)

If hard liquor is the choice, this is the one case where whiskey is spelled with an E . . . all other varieties are merely "whisky." The Irish specialty tastes quite different from Scotch, bourbon or rye; the best selections are aged at least seven years. (Poteen, another whiskey-type product is much stronger and illegal to make or drink.'

Another popular St. Patrick's day libation is Irish Coffee. While the Irish generally prefer tea, on important occasions this coffee-cum-whiskey drink is de rigeur.*

Once the parade is over (interestingly, Dublin often imports American bands for their own St. Patrick's Day marches), and after a toast or two or three . . . it's time to eat. To Americans, Irish food means corned beef and cabbage, but when I talked with my good friend Nora Blewitt, who is Irish-Irish, she looked a bit shocked at my suggestion of corned beef and accessories for a St. Patrick's day party. Evidently, that's a little bit like having hot dogs for Thanksgiving dinner. So with Nora's help we've come up with a menu that's eminently authentic and traditional . . . and more typical of what would be served on such an important occasion. Happily, enough of the dinner can be prepared in advance so that the hostess can enjoy the enthusiastic celebrating.

But consider a moment. What is the celebrating really *about?* Most Americans know two things about the patron saint of Ireland: 1. that his birthday is March 17; 2. that he chased the snakes out of Eire. Ironically, many scholars think there were at least *two* St. Patricks, and maybe even more since there are so many stories about him. One set of facts is fairly authenticated, however. There was a person named Magnus Sucatus Patricus, born in Britain about 386. His father was a Christian (originally from Rome), but young Patrick showed no interest in religion until he was about 16 when he was kidnapped by pirates and sold as a slave in what is now Northern Ireland. For a few years Patrick lived a quiet, meditative life as a shepherd and began to have visions of God.

At the age of 22 or so, he escaped to France and entered a monastery. It wasn't until he was about 46 that he went back to Ireland and began his legendary ministry. Folklore has it that the Druids, much more powerful then than the Christians, tried to kill him with poisoned wine, but Patrick froze the wine, poured off the poison, thawed the wine and then drank it.

And then there's the story of the snakes. Pat evidently had a big bass drum, and one day in an attempt to banish the vipers which were overrunning Ireland, he beat the drum so hard it burst. Miraculously, an angel appeared from the sky and patched the drum. The snakes, possibly overwhelmed by the cacophany, disappeared and have never been seen since in the Emerald Isle.

Another story associated with St. Patrick is how he used the shamrock to illustrate the significance of the Trinity. Trying to explain to the people about The Father, The Son and The Holy Ghost as three entities in one, St. Patrick bent down to pick up a shamrock, an appropriate example of the three-in-one principle. Ireland is the only place in the world, incidentally, where shamrocks will grow. Transplantation has defied the world's most eminent horticulturists.

For your own St. Patrick's day dinner party, try to emulate the traditional "Failte" (welcome) and plan your table setting to match the spirit of the authentic menu. More than the setting, however, is the atmosphere you establish. St. Patrick's Day is the time for singing Irish ballads ... and everybody seems to know some of them, ranging from "When Irish Eyes are Smiling" all the way through to "The Rose of Tralee." (Did you know in Ireland they even have a beauty contest to pick Miss Rose of Tralee?)

Irish records, featuring the songs of Carmel Quinn, Tommy Macom, the Ludlow Trio, the Irelanders, The Clancy Brothers, the Dubliners, the Chieftains, and the Wolf-Tones, are all good listening music during dinner, and later, the inspiration for everybody to sing. (If you have an enthusiastic pianist, plus an essential piano, an old-fashioned song-fest goes great with the Irish coffee.) Although we haven't included Irish Mist in our menu, if the party is going well and you want to keep the festivities moving, serve Irish Mist liqueur after the coffee. Spirits will really soar!

And spirit is what we're talking about. Despite a history of poverty and hard times, the prevailing Irish philosophy is one that we could all do well to live by: "I ndeireadh na scríbe beidgh gach rud go maith." Don't take things so seriously. Everything will work out well in the end!

On that note, as your guests take their first Irish whiskey cocktail, propose this toast:

> *"Health and long life to you.*
> *Land without rent to you.*
> *A child every year to you . . .*
> *And may you die in Ireland!*

# Gala St. Patrick's Day Dinner for 8

*Irish Mist Cocktails*                    *Hibernian Highballs*

## Appetizers

*Dublin Bay Prawns*                    *Smoked Salmon Galway*
*Irish Cheddar–Irish Blue Cheese
and Brown Bread*

## Soup

*Fergus Watercress Soup with Croutons*

## Main Course

*Roscommon Lamb Nessan with Mint Sauce*
*Croagh Patrick Potatoes*                    *Cabbage Tara*
*Lough Derg Minted Peas*                    *Bla Clieath Salad*
*Irish Soda Bread–Sweet Butter*

## Dessert

*Steamed Raisin Pudding with Whiskey Sauce*      *Irish Coffee*
*Guinness Stout with Dinner*
*(Optional: Irish Mist Liqueur after Dinner)*

# Irish Mist Cocktail

(A version of the drink called a Scotch Mist, not to be confused with Irish Mist liqueur).

*For Each Cocktail:*

3 ounces Irish Whiskey  
lemon peel  

shaved ice.  
old-fashioned glass.

Pour whiskey in glass; twist a strip of lemon peel over the glass to release oil; drop peel in glass. Add shaved ice and stir.

# Hibernian Highball

*For Each Cocktail:*

2 ounces Irish Whiskey  
ice cubes  

ginger ale or club soda  
tall glasses

Pour whiskey in glass; add ice cubes, fill with club soda or ginger ale. Stir.

# Dublin Bay Prawns

2 quarts water  
1 stalk celery, sliced  
1 carrot, sliced  
2 small onions, sliced  

*Sauce:*  
1 cup mayonnaise  
1 teaspoon malt or  
   tarragon vinegar

Juice of 1 lemon
2 teaspoons salt
1 teaspoon white pepper
1½ pounds prawns
  or jumbo shrimp,
  shelled and deveined

½ teaspoon Worcestershire
  sauce
1 teaspoon horseradish
.Salt and pepper to taste
½ cup whipped cream

**DAY BEFORE PARTY:**
1. In large saucepan bring 2 quarts of water to boil; add remaining ingredients, except shrimp, and boil for 20 minutes.
2. Add shrimp and simmer uncovered until pink and tender, 3 to 5 minutes. Drain and refrigerate.

**EARLY ON DAY OF PARTY:**
1. Arrange shrimp on serving platter, with room for sauce in the center.
2. Make sauce: mix all ingredients, except whipped cream together. When taste is adjusted, gently fold in whipped cream. Turn into serving bowl. Place on tray with shrimp. Cover with plastic wrap until serving time.

## Smoked Salmon Galway

1 pound thinly sliced
  smoked salmon
2 lemons cut in wedges
Sweet butter
Pepper mill

½ loaf Irish brown bread,
  cut in triangles, or
1 loaf of party rye

**AT SERVING TIME:**
1. Arrange salmon slices on a tray with lemon wedges and but-

tered triangles of brown bread (or rye). Serve with pepper mill nearby for those who want the added embellishment.

## *Cheese and Brown Bread*

½ pound Irish blue cheese
½ pound Irish cheddar

½ loaf of Irish brown bread,
   cut in triangles,
   or 1 loaf party rye
   or pumpernickel.

**DAY BEFORE PARTY:**
1. Cube cheese; arrange on serving plate; cover well with plastic wrap; refrigerate.

**AT SERVING TIME:**
1. Remove from refrigerator about 1 hour before serving; arrange on tray with brown bread, rye bread, or pumpernickel.

## *Fergus Watercress Soup*

4 tablespoons bacon grease
4 tablespoons butter
4 medium leeks,
   finely chopped
6 large potatoes,
   peeled and sliced
6 cups of chicken broth
   or stock

1 pound fresh watercress
   leaves
1 tablespoon salt
1 teaspoon white pepper
1 cup light cream
2 tablespoons chopped fresh
   fennel or 2 tablespoons
   fresh chopped parsley

**DAY BEFORE PARTY:**
1. Add bacon grease and 2 tablespoons of butter to a saucepan. Add leeks and sauté until transparent. Don't allow them to brown. Add potatoes, sauté together for five minutes.
2. Add 3 cups of stock to pan. Cook over medium heat until potatoes are just tender. Run through blender until smooth. Return to saucepan.
3. In another saucepan, melt 2 remaining tablespoons of butter, sauté the watercress for 2 or 3 minutes (don't let it brown), then add the 3 cups remaining stock and simmer gently for 10 minutes. Run the watercress mixture through the blender until smooth. Mix with potato mixture. Add salt and pepper. Cover and refrigerate overnight.

**AT SERVING TIME:**
1. Remove soup from refrigerator about 1 hour before dinner.
2. Over medium heat, bring potato-watercress mixture to a near boil (about 15 minutes).
3. When heated through, remove from stove, stir in light cream and fennel or parsley. Test for seasoning. Serve with buttered croutons.

## *Croutons*

4 slices white bread, trimmed          3 tablespoons butter
  of crusts

**EARLY ON DAY OF PARTY:**
1. Dice white bread in ½" cubes.
2. Melt butter in skillet; over low heat brown croutons on each side, for about 5 minutes.

3. Place in small aluminum foil pie tin. Cover and store at room temperature.

**AT SERVING TIME:**
1. Reheat croutons, covered, in 350° oven for 5 minutes.

## *Roscommon Lamb Nessan with Mint Sauce*

| | |
|---|---|
| 1  7 to 8 pound leg of lamb boned | 2 tablespoons butter |
| Salt and white pepper to taste | 1 garlic clove, minced |
| 1 teaspoon rosemary | 2 cups bread crumbs |
| 2 medium onions, sliced | ¼ cup chopped parsley |
| 2 tablespoons chopped scallions | ½ teaspoon thyme |

**ABOUT THREE HOURS BEFORE SERVING:**
1. Preheat over to 400°.
2. Sprinkle leg of lamb with salt, pepper, and rosemary.
3. Place sliced onions and scallions on bottom of roasting pan; place lamb on rack and bake for 2½ hours or until temperature registers 175° on a meat thermometer. If meat is cooking too fast, reduce heat to 350°. Baste meat with pan juices as it cooks. (If necessary, add a little water to bottom of pan.)
4. While meat is cooking, melt 2 tablespoons butter, sauté garlic for 2 minutes; then add bread crumbs, parsley and thyme to garlic mixture. Remove from heat.
5. When lamb is nearly done, pile breadcrumbs all over meat, baste with pan juices, cook another 5 minutes. Then remove

from oven and turn onto heated serving platter. Let sit 10 minutes. Carve at the table.

# Mint Sauce

4 tablespoons superfine sugar
2 teaspoons salt
½ cup boiling water

4 tablespoons finely chopped
  fresh mint
1½ cups malt or tarragon
  vinegar

**DAY BEFORE PARTY:**
1. Add sugar and salt to boiling water. Pour over mint; cover and steep for 5 minutes. Add vinegar and mix well. Let stand overnight.

**AT SERVING TIME:**
1. If desired, re-heat mint sauce slightly before turning into gravy boat. (Makes about 1½ cups sauce).

# Croagh Patrick Potatoes

8 large baking potatoes
½ cup cooked (crisp),
  diced bacon
1 stick of butter
4 tablespoons cheddar cheese

¼ cup chopped parsley
½ cup light cream
salt and pepper to taste
2 tablespoons butter

**DAY BEFORE PARTY:**
1. Bake potatoes.
2. When done, split in half, carefully reserving at least 12 shells;

discard the rest. Remove potato pulp; mash in a large bowl.
3. To the potatoes add chopped bacon, stick of butter, 2 table-spoons of grated cheese, parsley, light cream, salt and pepper to taste. Blend well.
4. Re-fill the shells. Sprinkle with remaining grated cheese. Dot with butter and refrigerate overnight.

**AT SERVING TIME:**
1. Remove potatoes from refrigerator about 1 hour before dinner.
2. Preheat oven to 350°. Heat potatoes for about 20 minutes or until heated through. Turn on broiler, broil potatoes for last 5 minutes or until cheese is melted and tops are golden brown.

# *Cabbage Tara*

4 tablespoons bacon fat
2 onions, finely chopped
1 large cabbage, halved,
  quartered then
  halved again

2 teaspoons salt
¼ teaspoon white pepper
4 tablespoons melted butter

**EARLY ON DAY OF PARTY:**
1. Heat bacon fat, add onions, brown lightly. Add the cabbage. Cover and steam for 10 minutes; cover with boiling water; and salt and pepper and cook until tender. Drain.
2. Pour melted butter over cabbage. Cover and set aside at room temperature.
**AT SERVING TIME:**
1. Reheat cabbage gently for about 5 minutes until warmed through.

# Lough Derg Minted Peas

½ cup chopped scallions
3 tablespoons butter
3 packages of tiny frozen
   green peas

4 tablespoons butter
1 tablespoon fresh or dry mint

**EARLY ON PARTY DAY:**
1. Sauté scallions in 3 tablespoons butter in small skillet. Set aside at room temperature.

**AT SERVING TIME:**
1. (Although you can't cook this ahead, if the scallions have been prepared, this dish takes just a few minutes.) Cook peas as directed on package, adding 4 tablespoons butter and mint to the cooking water. Drain well. Stir in scallions.

# Bla Clieath Salad

4 sliced tomatoes
1 cucumber, thinly sliced
1 1-lb can of sliced beets, well
   drained

4 hard-boiled eggs,
   peeled and quartered
crisp lettuce leaves

**EARLY ON PARTY DAY:**
1. On individual dishes, arrange tomatoes, cucumbers, beets, and 2 wedges of egg on a bed of lettuce. Cover each dish with plastic wrap and refrigerate. (If you don't have room to store assembled salads, prepare all ingredients and arrange before dinner.)

2. Prepare dressing:

1 cup salad oil
1 teaspoon salt
1 teaspoon sugar
1 teaspoon dry mustard

1 tablespoon finely chopped
 scallions
4 tablespoons malt or tarragon
 vinegar

Mix all ingredients in a covered glass jar. Set aside at room temperature.

**AT SERVING TIME:**
1. Shake dressing well and pour over cold salads.

## *Irish Soda Bread*

*For Two Loaves:*

2 pounds white flour
 (8 cups)
2 teaspoons salt
2 teaspoons sugar

½ teaspoon baking powder
2 cups buttermilk or
 sour milk*
3 tablespoons melted butter

**EARLY ON DAY OF PARTY:**
1. Preheat oven to 400°.
2. Sift dry ingredients together twice.
3. Add milk gradually, mixing well. The dough shouldn't be too dry.
4. Separate dough in half. Working with one half at a time, turn out on floured board and knead lightly just a few times.
5. Shape into a round flat loaf and cut a deep cross on top of loaf. Repeat with second mound of dough.
6. Bake on cookie sheet in 400° oven for 45 minutes (loaf should sound hollow when tapped).
7. When done, brush tops with melted butter. Cool on wire rack.

\* To make sour milk, remove 2 tablespoons of milk from the 2-cup measure and substitute 2 tablespoons of vinegar or lemon juice. Let mixture stand 10 minutes before using.

**AT SERVING TIME:**
1.  Cover bread with foil and place in heated oven for 10 minutes before serving with sweet butter.

## Steamed Raisin Pudding with Whiskey Sauce

*Pudding:*
3 cups milk
3 cups currents, or dark
  raisins, chopped
3 cups sifted flour
5 tablespoons baking powder
1⅓ cup sugar
1 teaspoon salt
2 teaspoons nutmeg
1 teaspoon cinnamon
6 eggs
3 cups bread crumbs
1 cup grated suet

*Whiskey Sauce:*
½ cup soft butter
4 cups brown sugar
2 eggs
2 cups light cream
¼ teaspoon nutmeg
½ cup Irish whiskey

**THREE HOURS BEFORE SERVING:**
1.  In double boiler top, heat milk and raisins 20 minutes over hot water. Remove from water; set aside for 15 minutes to cool.
2.  Sift flour with baking powder, sugar, salt, nutmeg, and cinnamon.
3.  In large bowl, beat eggs until light. Using electric mixer at low speed, beat in crumbs and suet until well mixed.
4.  At low speed, beat dry ingredients into egg mixture, alternating with milk mixture. Blend well.

5. Turn into greased 3-quart pudding mold (the type with a tube). Cover tightly with foil. Place on a trivet or rack in a large saucepan; add enough boiling water to reach half-way up side of mold.

6. With water bubbling and saucepan covered, steam for 2 hours. Remove pudding mold from water. Let stand about 10 minutes. (To serve, loosen pudding with knife, turn out of mold.)

7. Make whiskey sauce. In double boiler top, with electric mixer at medium speed, beat butter and sugar until creamy. Beat in eggs, cream, and nutmeg until mixture is fluffy. Cook, stirring now and then over hot, *not boiling*, water until thick. Remove from heat; stir in whiskey; set aside.

**AT SERVING TIME:**
1. Using double boiler, reheat sauce over hot, *not boiling* water for 5 minutes until warm.

# *Irish Coffee*

An old Irish saying gives the "ingredients" for this delectable beverage.

| | |
|---|---|
| **CREAM:** | rich as an Irish brogue |
| **COFFEE:** | strong as a friendly hand |
| **SUGAR:** | sweet as the tongue of a rogue |
| **WHISKEY:** | smooth as the wit of the land. |

Those are the basics, but more specifically, to serve 8 you need:
½ pint heavy cream, whipped to a froth, but not too stiff
12–16 cups of strong coffee (allow for seconds)
Sugar
12–16 ounces of Irish Whiskey

**AT SERVING TIME:**
1. Pour 1 ounce of Irish Whiskey into each of 8 heavy stemmed goblets or, if you're lucky enough to own them, Irish Coffee

cups. Then add 1 teaspoon of sugar and fill the goblet with coffee to within one inch of brim. Stir to mix coffee, whiskey, and sugar. Carefully add a good dollop of cream so it floats on top of the coffee in each glass and serve at once.

NOTE: To drink Irish coffee properly, the Irish insist that you do not stir after adding cream, since the true flavor of coffee and whiskey only comes through the coolness of the cream on top. In America we often add a few sprinkles of nutmeg to the cream, but this is not the custom in Ireland.

## *Expenses for a St. Patrick's Day Dinner for 8:*

| | |
|---|---|
| $ 6.75 | Irish Mist Cocktails |
| 4.50 | Hibernian Highballs |
| 5.90 | Dublin Bay Prawns |
| 5.00 | Smoked Salmon Galway |
| 2.20 | Irish Cheddar-Irish Blue Cheese |
| .30 | Brown Bread |
| 1.85 | Fergus-Watercress Soup with Croutons |
| 9.45 | Roscommon Lamb Nessan |
| .70 | Mint Sauce |
| 1.35 | Croagh Patrick Potatoes |
| .55 | Cabbage Tara |
| .95 | Lough Derg Minted Peas |
| 2.05 | Bla Clieath Salad |
| .55 | Irish Soda Bread/sweet butter |
| 4.00 | Steamed Raisin Pudding With Whiskey Sauce |
| 5.15 | Irish Coffee |
| 3.00 | Guinness Stout with dinner |
| $54.25 | |

This St. Patrick's Day Party with Irish Whiskey and stout plus Irish Coffee will cost approximately $6.75 per person.

# Summer-Outdoor Entertaining

## Enjoy a "Kef" (Good Time) with an Armenian Picnic for 12–16

In some ways Armenia is like Shangri-la—it doesn't really exist. What used to be a proud, expansive country embracing land from the Caucasus to the Mesopatamian Desert and from the Caspian Sea to the Mediterranean is now a small part of the fantastic spread of area called the U.S.S.R.

Through the centuries, Armenia had its own identity, but was over-run in turn by a dozen different empires, including the Romans, Turks, Persians and Mongols before Russia finally enveloped what was left of the beleaguered land as part of the Union of Soviet Socialist Republics in 1920.

But just as you can take the boy out of the country, but can't take the country out of the boy, you can take Armenia out of its realm as a separate entity, but you can't—really can't—demolish a very special, chauvinistic spirit that prevails and still strongly exists with Armenians, wherever in the world they happen to live.

Armenians still retain their language (actually an amalgam of Turkish, Russian, Armenian and other tongues), religious beliefs, and customs. Although the dances, vocabulary, and cuisine are a patchwork evolved from the many, many invasions their country lived through, there's still something very unique about Armenian culture.

And, significantly, whether born in their own part of the globe or Leonia, New Jersey, the traditions live on with a kind of persevering gaiety that commands respect from others whose national origins have not experienced as much turmoil.

If you're interested in the background of Armenian food and music, you have to take into consideration those invasions. Even the names of some Armenian dishes depend directly on who was invading the country when. For example, many Armenians in the 11th century were forced to move to Turkey where often they weren't allowed to speak their own language. (For this reason, so many Armenian dishes actually have Turkish names). One such is "Imam Bayaldi," a dish supposedly created when an Armenian housewife, surprised by a priest who dropped in uninvited for dinner, threw together whatever she had in the house: onions, tomatoes, garlic, olive oil and eggplant. When the priest tasted the first mouthful—"Iman bayaldi!"—he fainted, presumably from delight!

Ancient Armenia itself is not without tradition. This is the site of Mount Ararat, where Noah landed his ark. It's said that one of the first things he did was plant a vineyard. Although difficult to obtain the fruits of that vineyard today (given importation problems with the U.S.S.R.) many natural wines, fortified wines, and brandies are produced from that area, with more than 22,000 vineyard acres running all the way to the Caspian sea.

Then, too, Armenia was not without its place in classical history. The great historian, Plutarch, observed that "ancient Armenia was a land that abounded in plenty." Many early dishes call for wheat and fruit, staples which the inhabitants stored over the winter. In addition, Armenians were well into what has become a diet cult of modern Americans—yogurt. Called "madzoon" in Armenian culture, yogurt, plus whole wheat and dried fruit, was reputed to be a winning combination for longevity.

Armenians, very practically, adopted some customs of their invaders. Shish kebab, for example, was influenced by the Arabs, dolma was borrowed from the Turks. Lavash, the Armenian unleavened bread, however, is a fairly unique invention. Baked against the walls of an oven, lavash was then rolled into thin sheets before eating. A traditional Armenian greeting when someone comes to visit is "Let us break bread in friendship."

Armenians love the land and fully enjoy basic, natural foods. Cheese is a great favorite, including a marvelous blue cheese, plus Tel-Bani, a cheese that's shredded before eating. Armenians eat cheese at dinner as a first course . . . and often with fruit for dessert. Armenians know how to live and can turn ordinary occasions into celebrations. In their native land, the mountain streams and banks provide an ideal setting for picnics, and when the weather is fair, this is where Armenians head . . . for the mountains. Traditionally, they take along live lambs (to make the shish kebab) plus lavash, vegetables for salad, cheese, homemade vodka and "oghie" (the anise-tasting white firewater whisky taken either straight or, here in America, on the rocks). There isn't any religious significance to the sacrifice of the lambs, but actually Armenians are following the custom of ancient Christians in slaughtering lambs at the place of feasting.

Aside from eating, Armenians have a rich repertoire of dances ritually performed to celebrate the occasion—any occasion. There's the "butchari," an Armenian circle dance, the "shourtch," done in a line holding pinky fingers, the "chefte telli" (solo dances) where everyone does his own thing, and the men's dances done with many knee bends and hand-kerchiefs, much like the Greek exercises in machismo.

Okay, so how can you emulate the Armenian atmosphere, aside from shish kebab and the rest of the authentic dishes included in the recipe section? For one thing, obtain some typical records, which actually give a lot of the Turkish and Arabic flavor as well as the Armenian customs. A good one to start with is called "Rendezvous" (Roulette records #R-25-230). Then, while you're having your Armenian picnic fare, listen to the *oud* artistry of John Berberian. (Mainstream records #S 6047). After lunch it's time to do some Armenian folk dancing.

For your American-Armenian "Tashdahantess" (literally Tash = outdoors, and dahantess = a big dance), try to obtain the records through stores or your public library; then track down a Near-Eastern or Armenian-Greek specialty store which will carry all the ethnic products you need for a grand banquet.

This Armenian picnic is one of the best examples of preparing food in advance. A good many dishes are served cold . . . the ones that need your attention won't take atmosphere away from the party. While you cover the oven for 5 to 10 minutes, your guests will be enjoying their oghie, trying a dance step, and generally having a "kef"—the Armenian way of saying a "GOOD TIME"!

# Armenian Picnic for 12–16

*Oghie (either straight as an apèritif, or on the rocks)*     *Beer*

### Appetizers

*Pasterma*
*(Dried, Spiced Beef)*

*Plaki Fousula*
*(Bean Salad)*

*Yalanchi Dolma*
*(Stuffed Grape Leaves)*

*Jajik*
*(Yogurt Cucumber Salad)*

*Tel-Bani Cheese-Tomato-Olive Tray*

*Lavash*
*(Armenian Flat Bread)*

### Main Course

*Shish Kebab*
*(Lamb on Skewers)*

*Pilaf*
*(Armenian Rice)*

*Lavash Bread*

*Patlijan Salata*
*(Egg Plant Salad)*

*Tahn (Yogurt Drink)*

### Desserts

*Beoreg Khenzhor*
*(Apple Pastries)*

*Beoreg Enguyz*
*(Walnut Pastries)*

*Armenian Coffee*

# *Pasterma*
## *(Dried, Spiced Beef)*

Arrange 1 pound of Pasterma (cut in very thin slices) on a tray. Fold or roll each slice of beef for attractive appearance as well as easy handling for finger food with pieces of Lavash.

# *Yalanchi Dolma*
## *(Stuffed Grape Leaves)*

8 onions
1 cup olive oil
1 cup *short* grain rice
   such as River brand
1 cup water (boiling)
1 tablespoon salt
2 tablespoons tomato paste

1 bunch curly parsley,
   chopped fine
½ cup lemon juice
¼ teaspoon each of cinna-
   mon, nutmeg, allspice
1 16-ounce jar grape leaves
4 teaspoons butter
lemon wedges for garnish

**DAY BEFORE PARTY:**
1. Cook onions in olive oil until soft and golden, not brown.
2. Stir rice into water. Cover and cook 15 minutes until water is absorbed. Rice will not be completely cooked. Stir in salt, tomato paste, parsley, lemon juice and spices. Cook another minute or two.
3. Now assemble dolma (make about 50). With the vein side of the leaf facing you, remove the stem. Add ½ teaspoon of rice mixture just above the point where stem was removed. Fold the top part of the leaf on each side diagonally across to cover the rice. Then roll toward the other end of the leaf—make one roll and tuck in the sides, roll again and

tuck in the sides. Tuck the bottom edge in neatly. You should have a tight roll. Practice a few times until you master the technique.

4. Line the bottom of a large heavy pot or cast iron casserole with a layer of grape leaves (if anything burns it will be the extra leaves, not the dolma.) Then place the rolled dolma close together in layers. Pour 1 cup of boiling water over dolma. Dot with 4 teaspoons of butter and cover dolma with an inverted aluminum foil pie pan to keep them in place.

5. Cover saucepan and cook at high heat just until you hear the water inside the pot bubbling. Lower heat and cook 45 minutes longer. The dolma should be fork tender. Let them sit on the stove a few hours. Then place in an attractive serving dish and refrigerate until party.

**AT SERVING TIME:**
1. Serve the dolma cold garnished with lemon wedges.

# *Plaki Fousula*
## *(Bean Salad)*

**DAY BEFORE PARTY:**
In a serving bowl combine 2 1 lb. cans of Cannellini beans, drained; 3–4 ripe tomatoes, chopped; 1 bunch of scallions, chopped; 1 bunch of parsley, chopped; 1 large green pepper, diced; ½ cup olive oil; ¼ cup of wine vinegar, 1 tablespoon salt. Mix together gently. Taste to correct seasoning and oil and vinegar. Refrigerate until serving time; garnish with green pepper rings.

# Jajik
## (Yogurt-Cucumber Salad)

**DAY OR TWO BEFORE PARTY:**
*MAKE MADZOON (YOGURT):*
1 quart homogenized whole milk
4 tablespoons plain yogurt. (If you can, get madzoon from an Armenian food shop or other specialty food store; if not, use commercial plain yogurt)

1. In a two-quart stainless steel or teflon-lined pan, scald milk by cooking over low to medium heat for 20 to 30 minutes. (Not high heat: milk will burn!) You'll know it's done if you take it off the stove just as milk starts to foam up. Then let it cool for 15 minutes.
2. Pour scalded milk into two pint-sized glass jars with covers. Let cool in jars until a finger dipped in doesn't "pinch." The temperature should be about the same as that for a good hot bath, not burning, but not lukewarm, either. (If you have a kitchen thermometer, 100° is the ideal temperature.) At this point add 2 tablespoons of "old" yogurt to each bottle, blend in well. Cover the jars tightly.
3. Place jars on a bath-sized towel and envelop completely. Let stand, wrapped in the towel for 5 to 7 hours. Check at 5 hours. If the yogurt has "caked," then it's time to refrigerate the batch. The longer the yogurt sits unrefrigerated, the tarter it will be, so go by your own taste buds on this one. (Incidentally, always remember to save 4 tablespoons from each batch of yogurt to make a new batch—this is called the "starter".) Note: If you'd rather skip making your own madzoon, either buy two pints in an Armenian food shop, or buy 2 pints of the plain commercial yogurt in the supermarket for the following recipe:

**EARLY ON DAY OF PARTY:**
1. Pour 2 pints of madzoon into mixing bowl. Add 3 pared, sliced and quartered cucumbers, ½ cup of dried mint, ½ teaspoon garlic powder and salt to taste. Blend gently. Refrigerate until serving time.

## Tel-Bani Cheese-Tomato-Olive Tray

1 pound of Tel-Bani cheese
1 pound of Greek or Italian cured olives
1 pint of cherry tomatoes

**EARLY ON DAY OF PARTY:**
1. Open up the Tel-Bani cheese and pull it in long strings. Refrigerate until just before serving.

**AT SERVING TIME:**
1. Place Tel-Bani in cold water for 5 minutes. Drain well. Arrange on serving tray with olives and cherry tomatoes; serve with Lavash.

## Shish Kebab
### (Lamb on Skewers)

8 pounds of boned lamb, cut in 1½" cubes
2 cups red wine
Juice from 2 lemons
½ cup olive oil
4 cloves garlic, crushed
2 tablespoons salt
freshly ground black pepper
2 teaspoons oregano.

1 box cherry tomatoes (or 5 or 6 under-ripe tomatoes, cut in wedges)
3 green peppers, cut in rectangular slices
48–60 small white onions, peeled
36 large mushroom caps (freeze the stems for another use)

**DAY BEFORE PARTY:**
1. Check the lamb and remove any bits of fat or gristle the butcher may have missed. (Incidentally, you can save money if you have the time and patience and skill to bone-out two legs of lamb.)
2. In a large bowl, mix together the wine, lemon juice, olive oil, garlic, salt, pepper and oregano. Add the lamb and marinate overnight in the refrigerator, turning lamb pieces several times to make sure they all get doused in the liquid.
3. The next morning, add the vegetables, mixing in very gently.

**AT SERVING TIME:**
1. About an hour before guests arrive, assemble the kebabs on individual skewers, alternating meat with various vegetables. Reserve left-over marinade. Place kebabs on a large tray or trays. Cover with plastic wrap and store at room temperature or cool place until time to grill.
2. Grill about 4–6 inches above gray-white hot coals for about 15 minutes, turning once and basting frequently with reserved marinade.

# *Pilaf*
## *(Armenian Rice)*

3 sticks of butter
1½ cups thin egg noodles

3 cups long-grain rice
2 tablespoons salt

**THIRTY MINUTES BEFORE SERVING:**
1. In a 4-quart saucepan, melt the butter, add egg noodles and saute lightly until golden.
2. Add rice, blend with the noodles. Add 6 cups of water, the salt and let mixture come to boil. About 2 minutes later, cover tightly, lower heat and cook 20 minutes or until water is absorbed and rice is tender. Serve hot.

# *Patlijan Salata*
## *(Eggplant Salad)*

2 large eggplants
1 bunch chopped parsley
3 medium sized, ripe
   tomatoes, chopped
1 green pepper, diced
1 bunch scallions, diced

1 tablespoon salt
¼ cup olive oil
¼ cup wine vinegar
1 teaspoon garlic powder
1 pimiento for garnish

**DAY BEFORE PARTY:**
1. Prick eggplants with fork. Place in a roasting pan and bake in a 350° oven for 1½ hours or until tender.
2. Scoop out the pulp (discard skin), mash with a fork or potato ricer until mixture is coarsely mashed. Add parsley, tomatoes, pepper, scallions, salt, oil, vinegar, and garlic powder. Taste for seasoning. Garnish with pimiento. Refrigerate until serving time.

# *Tahn*
## *(Yogurt Drink)*

2 pints madzoon (either make it yourself, or buy commercial variety)
2 quarts water
Ice

**AT SERVING TIME:**
1. When you're ready to serve the main course, add 1 pint of madzoon to each of two pitchers; then add 1 quart of water to each pitcher; stir well. Pour into ice-cube filled glasses If yogurt settles, stir madzoon-water mixture up again vigorously.

# Beoreg Khenzhor–Beoreg Enguyz
## (Apple Pastries & Walnut Pastries)

**Apple Filling:**
⅓ cup ground almonds or
  pecans
1 teaspoon cinnamon
10 apples, peeled, cored
  and diced
¾ cup sugar

**Walnut Filling:**
2 pounds of walnuts,
  chopped in blender
2 teaspoons almond extract
1 cup confectioners sugar
½ cup honey

**Pastry** (enough for both types of boereg):
1 pound phyllo sheets
½ pound sweet butter (or more)

**A WEEK BEFORE PARTY:**
1. Prepare each of the fillings by mixing listed ingredients together.

*ASSEMBLE BEOREG:*

1. Remove one sheet of phyllo (cover remaining sheets with damp cloth to keep moist). Brush with melted butter. Fold the two sides of the sheet evenly toward the middle. Fold over lengthwise once again. You now have a long strip of 4 thicknesses of pastry. Brush with butter.
2. Place 1 teaspoon of filling at the end of the strip nearest you, flattening filling out slightly. Take the right hand corner of the pastry and fold it in a triangle to meet the left side. Then, with the left side, make an angle over to the right side. Continue folding in this right-left angle fashion until the end of the strip. Tuck the bottom edge inside the triangular folds. Makes about 20 nut beoreg, 20 apple beoreg.
3. Place pastries on a cookie sheet. If you have a large plastic bag, slip this over the tray; otherwise wrap well in plastic wrap. Cover with aluminum foil and freeze.

**AT SERVING TIME:**
1. Preheat oven to 350°.
2. Remove beoreg from freezer, uncover, and cook for half an hour until pastries are golden and puffy.

# Armenian Coffee

*For 30 Demitasse Cups:*
8 cups of water
6 teaspoons sugar
10 tablespoons Greek or Turkish coffee

**AT SERVING TIME:**
1. In a 9 or 10 cup coffee pot, add water, sugar and coffee. Stir until blended. Heat over high temperature until mixture comes to a boil. Remove from heat. The top part of the coffee that is still bubbling is called the "Kaïmak"—the cream—of the coffee. Add a little "kaïmak" to 16 demi-tasse cups, then pour more coffee in each cup.
2. For seconds, bring coffee to a boil again to create more "kaïmak," and refill cups.

# Expenses for an Armenian Picnic for 12–16:

| | |
|---|---|
| $ 7.00 | Oghie (straight or on the rocks) |
| 5.00 | Beer (one case) |
| 4.50 | Pasterma (dried, spiced beef) |
| 2.60 | Yalanchi Dolma (stuffed grape leaves) |
| 1.75 | Plaki Fousula (bean salad) |
| .95 | Jajik (yogurt-cucumber salad) |
| 3.40 | Tel-Bani Cheese-Tomatoes-Olives Tray |

| | |
|---|---|
| 2.25 | Lavash (bread for both appetizers and main course) |
| 22.00 | Shish Kebab (lamb on skewers) |
| 1.15 | Pilaf (Armenian rice) |
| 2.15 | Patlijan Salata (Eggplant salad) |
| .30 | Tahn (yogurt drink)* |
| 2.35 | Beoreg Khenzhor (apple pastries) |
| 3.10 | Beoreg Enguzy (walnut pastries) |
| 1.30 | Armenian Coffee |
| $59.80 | |

Invite your friends to have a unique picnic, Armenian style, for $3.75 a person.

*(\*If home-made yogurt; commercial yogurt costs about $1.00)*

119

# Take a Fantasy Trip with a
# South Seas Island Party for 20–25

Romantic. Exotic. Idyllic. The islands of the South Seas inspire these descriptions and more. If you can't make the real trip to Hawaii or Tahiti, bring the islands to you with a swinging summertime party that combines authenticity with gala festivities.

Everyone is familiar with the Hawaiian luau, but for your own island fête, combine the best of Hawaii and Tahiti. A Tahitian version of a luau is called a "tamaaraa." The food for both events is fairly similar since the islands have the same native ingredients to choose from. Equally important, however, both cuisines show the influences of foreigners and traders—the Chinese, Japanese, Portuguese, French, British, and Americans, who have lent their customs and traditions to the entire Polynesian area.

As unbelievable as it sounds, it was the Americans who introduced pineapples and sugar to Hawaii! The Chinese brought over noodles and long rice, ginger, black beans and water chestnuts; the Japanese contributed the hibachi, sashimi, tempura and the firewater called sake. The Portuguese transported their favorite way of seasoning dishes with tomatoes, onions, green peppers. The French influence in Tahiti comes through in some of the Tahitian music and several distinctive approaches to cooking, while the British lent their interest in rum and some very English puddings!

Although the food at a luau and tamaaraa has a definite kinship, other traditions vary. Hawaiians decorate their luau more lavishly than the Tahitians who favor plain wooden tables. But the tamaaraa is a livelier affair, featuring more exciting music. Tahitians also dance more vivaciously than the Hawaiians who love the undulant variations of the hula dance.

Set the atmosphere for your island adventure—and get the guests in groove—by sending invitations with a bon voyage theme... or find a card with exotic orchids or gardenias on it. Since this should be a sort of journey in fantasy, give added dimension by asking guests to come dressed as island celebrities in fact or fiction: Gauguin, Bloody Mary or Nellie Forbish of the Musical *South Pacific,* Mr. Christian, Captain Bligh and sailors of the "Bounty," Sadie Thompson and her minister, Dorothy Lamour in a sarong. Those who can't think of a specific character will certainly get in the mood with muumuus for the girls and wild, flowered Truman-esque shirts for the men.

The invitation might read:

**TAKE A TRIP TO THE SOUTH SEAS**

**WITH ROB AND MARY GILMOUR ON**

Saturday Night, July 11th.

**DEPARTURE TIME: 8:00 p.m.**

**PIER: 84 Summit Street, Clifton**

**TRAVEL AS YOUR FAVORITE FACTUAL OR FICTIONAL**

**SOUTH SEAS PERSONALITY**

R.S.V.P.—489-0034

Check the long-range weather forecast (for hope, if nothing else), pray to the Sun-God, and then plan to decorate your own back yard and patio to approximate a tropical island. Your budget has to be the guide here, but you could include aloha lamps or Japanese lanterns strung among the trees, lots of inexpensive citronella candles in webbed glass holders, flowers and masses of greenery.

If you have a pool, float magnolias (they can be fake, if you like) on the surface. Ti leaves—those broad, shiny, dark-green leaves indigenous to the islands—are used for both decorative serving as well as cooking. These may be hard to come by and/or expensive, but you can substitute ferns, palm leaves, hydrangea or caladium leaves which are more readily available.

Forget about standard table and chair set-ups. You can deviate from custom by having your buffet table at a normal height (in Hawaii it would be just inches from the ground), but then let guests eat where they will at any of five or six little groupings complete with cushions stolen from lawn furniture, borrowed from friends, or improvised with bed pillows. At each eating center, place a small bowl or sea shell filled with red Hawaiian salt and a bowl of macadamia nuts.

Cover the main buffet table with the brightest, splashiest cloth you can find. Make one out of wild cotton print, or buy a vividly flowered sheet. Remember, vibrant color is typical of both Hawaii and Tahiti. Don't be afraid to get really lavish and exotic! Then place broad leaves decoratively around the table to continue the island atmosphere.

You can add to the authenticity by picking up paper leis, spirit lamps, artificial shells, etc., in the import "bazaar" shops which carry such items, often very inexpensively.

The traditional luau always includes Kalua pig baked under ground in an "imu." Since you probably don't want to tear up your backyard to recreate the authentic imu, instead of the whole porker, we've substituted pork loin. No luau is complete without Lomi Salmon and Haupia (a coconut pudding), both of which we've included. We have, however, eliminated poi, a grayish paste made by fermenting roasted taro roots: it's difficult to obtain even the canned version here . . . and it's not particularly a taste threat if you haven't been schooled in it previously.

At a "real" luau, everyone pitches in to build the oven, catch the fish, arrange flowers. Unfortunately, our American version eliminates these steps, but I can't help thinking what fun a joint effort would be. The next step, however, follows tradition. While the feast cooks in Hawaii or Tahiti, everyone watches the dancing and enjoys a drink ... or two ... or three ... while nibbling on the many "pupus" (hors d'oeuvres) served to keep appetites up and sobriety more or less in control. (In Hawaii fermented liquor was originally enjoyed by priests and chiefs. When traders came they taught islanders how to make what is now the national drink, a distilled liquor from the ti plant called "okolehao.")

Tahitians would enjoy various rum drinks while watching and participating in the frenetic dancing. For our combined luau-tamaaraa we've included a potent rum punch, meant to be appreciated through the entire party, a drink that will make hula dancers out of the most reticent guests.

In fact, before serving the main course, why not arrange two dance competitions? One for the more upbeat Tahitian music, another for the Hawaiian symbolic swaying. Your public library can supply a good selection of Tahitian, Hawaiian, and Polynesian music in general. Several records that will work well for the entire evening are "Blue Hawaiian Waters" (Coronet CXS 128), Rank Chacksfield's "Hawaii" (London SP 44087), and Leroy Holmes' "Music of Hawaii" (Metro M590).

Of course your best dancers deserve prizes and you should also reward the best costumes, perhaps at an after dinner prize awarding event. Likely trophies might include a copy of *Mutiny on the Bounty* or Michener's *Hawaii* or *Tales of the South Pacific,* or prints of Gauguin classics.

Now that you have the setting, here's the menu for an unforgettable bash ... one that will earn you kudos (if not a lei) as a really imaginative hostess.

# South Seas Island Party for 20–25

### Pupus
### (Hors D'Oeuvres)

Teriyaki on Skewers                                    Lomi Salmon

Islander Shrimp with Orange-Ginger Sauce                Rumaki

Macadamia Nuts

### Main Course

Roast Loin of Pork, Polynesian              Chicken Tahitian

Planked Fish, Baked in Coconut Sauce

Glazed Sweet Potatoes with Macadamia Nuts

Baked Bananas                                        Rice Papeete

### Desserts

Haupia (Coconut Pudding)          Pineapple Snow Pudding

Daiquiri Chiffon Pie                              Fresh Fruit

Rum Punch ... and ... Fruit Punch before and after dinner

# Island Rum Punch

3 bottles light rum
3 bottles dark Jamaica rum
½ pound sugar-in-the-raw
   or brown sugar
2 whole vanilla beans
18 oranges
18 lemons
3 limes

3 large grapefruit
1 ripe pineapple
3 ripe bananas
2 bottles dry white wine,
   chilled
Slioed fruit and flowers for
   garnish

**THREE DAYS BEFORE PARTY:**
1. Pour rum into a 4-gallon keg, crock, or stainless steel pot. (Don't use aluminum or other metal container.) Add sugar and vanilla beans. Stir until sugar dissolves.
2. Cut oranges, lemons, limes and grapefruit in half. Squeeze the juice into rum mixture, then add the citrus halves to keg. Peel, core and slice pineapple, slice bananas and add both fruits to rum mixture.
3. Let the punch sit for 3 days, stirring 3 or 4 times a day.

**AT SERVING TIME:**
1. Remove fruit and citrus rinds. Pour rum over ice in large punch bowl. Just before serving add the chilled wine. If you don't have a punch bowl and don't want to rent one; remove fruit and rind as above, add ice and chilled wine to keg. Decorate punch with sliced fruit and some flowers. (About 3 4-ounce drinks of punch per guest.)

# Pineapple Fruit Punch

2 cups sugar
1 quart water

2 quarts pineapple juice
2 quarts club soda
   or ginger ale

1 cup strained lemon juice
1 quart Hawaiian punch
1 6-ounce can orange juice
 concentrate

Pineapple slices for garnish
Whole strawberries (garnish)
Mint sprigs (garnish)

**EARLY ON DAY OF PARTY:**
1. Combine sugar and water. Cook until it becomes a thin, syrupy mixture.
2. In large (about 6 quarts) stainless steel pot or glass container, mix syrup with lemon juice, Hawaiian punch, orange juice concentrate and pineapple juice. Set aside.

**AT SERVING TIME:**
1. In a punch bowl or other suitable container, add 1 large block of ice, plus the club soda or ginger ale and the fruit juice mixture. Garnish with pineapple slices, strawberries and mint. (Makes about 6 quarts of punch or 48 4-ounce servings)

## Teriyaki on Skewers

*For Teriyaki:*
3 pounds of ½" thick sirloin
 tip steak

3 dozen bamboo skewers
 (available in import shops)

*For Marinade:*
1½ cups soy sauce
½ cup sherry
3 cloves garlic, crushed

1 medium onion, chopped
2 inches root ginger, crushed

**DAY BEFORE PARTY:**
1. Cut sirloin into thin strips. Place 1 strip of beef on each skewer. If you can't find bamboo skewers, use small metal skew-

ers used to truss poultry, or long pieces of thick wire, curved with a little handle at the end.
2. Place prepared skewers in shallow dish.
3. Mix together ingredients for marinade and pour over meat. Refrigerate overnight.

## AT COOKING TIME:
1. Make a charcoal fire. When coals are gray-white, place skewers close together in a sausage-grill (reserve marinade for dipping) and broil quickly about 2 minutes each side.
2. Remove from grill; turn into large platter; have napkins handy so guests can grasp end of skewers without burning fingers. Serve with reserved marinade as a dip.

## *Lomi Salmon*

1½ pounds smoked or salted
  salmon
½ teaspoon sugar
2 teaspoons salt
5 dashes tabasco sauce

¾ cup chopped onions
Juice of 6 limes
4 cups diced,
  peeled tomatoes
Chopped chives

## EARLY ON DAY OF PARTY:
1. If using salted salmon, wipe salmon with damp cloth; cover with water; soak 2 or 3 hours.
2. Remove skin and bones from salmon; dice and put in stainless steel or ceramic bowl. Add sugar, salt, Tabasco sauce, onions, and lime juice and marinate for 6 hours in refrigerator, stirring occasionally.
3. Meanwhile, chill tomatoes. When ready to serve, combine salmon with tomatoes and mix well. Serve in small shells, or little dishes. Add chopped chives for garnish.

## *Islander Shrimp Luau with Orange-Ginger Sauce*

60 raw jumbo shrimp (about
   3 pounds, shelled
   and deveined
½ cup lemon juice
1 teaspoon salt
3 teaspoons curry powder

½ teaspoon ginger
4 cups flour
2⅔ cups milk
4 teaspoons baking powder
Shaved, toasted coconut
Fat for deep frying

**EARLY ON DAY OF PARTY:**
1. Split shrimp lengthwise with sharp knife, but don't cut entirely through. Combine lemon juice, salt, curry powder and ginger and marinate shrimp in mixture for several hours. Then drain shrimp; reserve marinade.
2. Mix flour, milk and baking powder thoroughly. Add marinade to batter.
3. Dredge shrimp with additional flour, dip in batter and roll in shaved, toasted coconut. Fry in deep fat at 375° until golden brown, four to six minutes. Drain on paper towels. Turn into roasting pan. Cover with foil. Refrigerate.

**AT SERVING TIME:**
1. Remove shrimp from refrigerator 1 hour before serving.
2. Heat quickly in 350° oven for 5 minutes or until heated through.

## *Orange Ginger Sauce*

2 tablespoons butter
2 tablespoons cornstarch
3 tablespoons soy sauce

¼ cup sherry
2 teaspoons slivered orange
   peel

1 cup orange juice
¼ cup vinegar
¼ cup sugar

Finely chopped crystallized
 ginger

**EARLY ON DAY OF PARTY:**
1. Melt butter in saucepan. Mix cornstarch with soy sauce to make a paste. Add remaining ingredients to pan and thicken with the paste. Cook 5 minutes or longer, until sauce is clear and thick.
2. Cover and store at room temperature.

**AT SERVING TIME:**
1. While shrimp is reheating, warm sauce over low heat.

## *Rumaki*

¼ pound butter
30 chicken livers (1½ pounds)

30 canned water chestnuts
15 slices of bacon, cut in half

**EARLY ON DAY OF PARTY:**
1. Melt butter in skillet. Sauté chicken livers in butter until golden; then cool. For each rumaki, wrap 1 chicken liver and 1 drained water chestnut with ½ bacon slice; skewer with toothpick. Refrigerate.

**AT SERVING TIME:**
1. Place nibblers in sausage grate; then broil on grill until bacon is crisp. Serve very hot, on toothpicks.

# Roast Loin of Pork, Polynesian

**Pork:**
2 4-pound pork loins, boned
4 tablespoons chopped crys-
.tallized ginger
½ cup soy sauce
Watercress for garnish

**Glaze:** mix together:
¼ cup soy sauce
½ teaspoon ginger
1 6-ounce can frozen pineapple juice concentrate
1 tablespoon lemon juice
1 tablespoon mustard
¼ cup honey or brown sugar

**EARLY ON PARTY DAY:**
1. Preheat oven to 325°.
2. With paring knife, make slits at intervals in each pork loin. Insert ginger in slits in each roast (about 1 tablespoon ginger per roast.)
3. Combine remaining ginger and soy sauce (not from the glaze).
4. Place pork loins, fat side up in shallow roasting pan, without rack. Insert meat thermometer in center of one loin.
5. Brush pork with part of soy sauce mixture. Cook about 2 hours or until meat thermometer reads 180°. (Baste with soy sauce mixture several times.)
6. Remove from oven. Cool slightly. Cover with foil and refrigerate. If you are serving within 3 hours, store at room temperature.

**AT SERVING TIME:**
1. Preheat oven to 350°.
2. Cover pork loins with glaze. Cook for 20 minutes.
3. Remove from oven. Let sit 10 or 15 minutes before carving.
4. Serve on a wood board on a bed of watercress. Carve at the table.

# Chicken Tahitian

5 chicken breasts, split and
boned
10 legs and thighs
1 cup unsifted flour
2 teaspoons salt
2 teaspoons ginger

½ teaspoon pepper
½ cup cooking oil
½ cup butter
1 1-lb. can of crushed pineapple, undrained
4 teaspoons soy sauce
1 cup water

**DAY BEFORE OR EARLY ON PARTY DAY:**
1. Wipe chicken with damp paper towels.
2. In a clean paper bag, combine flour, salt, ginger and pepper.
Add a few pieces of chicken at a time to bag and shake, coating
well.
3. Heat oil and butter in large skillet. Add enough chicken
pieces just to fit (don't overlap). Brown well, turning once or
twice. Set browned chicken aside; continue cooking until all
chicken is brown. Then return all chicken pieces to skillet.
4. In small bowl, combine pineapple, soy sauce, and water;
pour over chicken.
5. Cover, simmer 30 minutes or until chicken is fork tender.
Let cool to room temperature; refrigerate.

**AT SERVING TIME:**
1. Remove from refrigerator 1 hour before dinner.
2. Reheat at low temperature 20 minutes until warmed through.

# Planked Fish Baked in Coconut Sauce

5 pound red snapper, boned
Kosher salt

2 oranges, peeled and sectioned

1 cup coconut cream (see recipe following)
2 tablespoons sherry
2 lemons, sliced
1 grapefruit, peeled and sectioned

4 pineapple slices, quartered
1 small can green seedless grapes, drained, or handful of fresh grapes

**ONE HOUR BEFORE PARTY:**
1. Preheat oven to 350°.
2. Rub snapper with kosher salt.
3. Place fish in shallow baking dish and pour coconut cream over it.
4. Bake in oven for 20 to 25 minutes, then pour sherry over fish.
5. Continue baking 20 minutes longer, basting frequently with pan juices. Fish is cooked when it flakes easily with fork.

**AT SERVING TIME:**
1. Place fish on plank. Border with lemon slices, grapefruit and orange sections, pineapple segments and grapes.

## Coconut Cream

2 large or 3 medium-sized coconuts
About 2 quarts of milk

**DAY BEFORE PARTY:**
1. Preheat oven to 375°.
2. With an ice pick or strong nail, puncture two holes in each of the coconuts, drain and reserve any liquid.
3. Bake the drained coconuts for 20 minutes.
4. Then tap the coconuts with a hammer until the shells fall off. Remove the dark outer skin with a vegetable parer, rinse

with water and cut white meat into half inch chips or chunks. Measure the chunks. You should have about 7 or 8 cups of coconut meat.

5. Measure the amount of coconut liquid reserved. This liquid when combined with milk should equal the number of cups of coconut meat. Scald the amount of milk you need and mix it with coconut liquid.

6. In a blender, mix one cup of coconut-scalded milk and 1 cup of coconut cubes. Blend for 30–40 seconds. Empty blender into large bowl and keep repeating blending procedure until liquid and coconut cubes are all combined.

7. Drain mixture through cheesecloth or terry towel, squeezing out as much liquid as possible. (Save the shredded coconut for other uses). The resulting 7–8 cups will be enough for the Planked Fish recipe, above, and the Haupia dessert on page 135. Refrigerate Coconut Cream until needed.

## Glazed Sweet Potatoes with Macadamia Nuts

12 sweet potatoes, boiled
2 cups dark brown sugar
1 cup honey
6 tablespoons water

1 stick butter
1 tablespoon grated lemon rind
1 cup chopped macadamia nuts

**DAY BEFORE PARTY:**
1. Preheat oven to 350°.
2. Peel potatoes, halve and quarter them and place in baking dish.
3. Combine sugar, honey, water, butter and lemon rind in saucepan. Bring mixture to boil and pour over sweet potatoes.
4. Bake for 15 minutes, basting several times. Cool to room temperature and refrigerate.

**AT SERVING TIME:**
1. Remove casserole from refrigerator 1 hour before dinner.
2. Preheat oven to 350°.
3. Bake for 10 minutes until bubbling. Remove from oven and sprinkle with nuts.

## Baked Bananas in Orange Juice

16 medium-sized, under-ripe bananas, with slightly green skins
2 medium-sized oranges, peeled and cut in chunks
½ cup orange juice
4 tablespoons lemon juice
½ cup brown sugar
1 teaspoon cinnamon
¼ teaspoon nutmeg

**HALF AN HOUR BEFORE SERVING:**
1. Preheat oven to 350°.
2. Peel bananas; cut neatly in half lengthwise and arrange in shallow baking dish. Combine remaining ingredients and pour over bananas.
3. Bake 20 to 25 minutes or until bananas are golden and tender. Keep hot on food warmer until ready to serve or reheat briefly in low oven until sauce is bubbling.

## Rice Papeete

4½ cups raw long-grain white rice
2 sticks of butter
2 teaspoons cinnamon
1 teaspoon powdered saffron
2 tablespoons salt
1 cup golden raisins, soaked in 1 cup hot water for 10 minutes to plump.
½ cup macadamia nuts
½ cup diced green pepper

**DAY BEFORE PARTY:**
1. Soak rice in 3 quarts of cold water for half an hour; then drain well.
2. Melt butter in an 8 or 9-quart heavy saucepan; add rice, sauté, stirring for 3 minutes.
3. In another saucepan, combine 9 cups of water with cinnamon, saffron and salt. Bring to boiling; boil 3 minutes.
4. Pour seasoned water over rice and cook, covered, until rice is tender and all water is absorbed. About 15 minutes.
5. Add raisins, nuts, and green pepper. Cool to room temperature. Refrigerate overnight.

**AT SERVING TIME:**
1. Remove rice from refrigerator about 1 hour before dinner.
2. Add ½ cup of water to rice, blending in gently.
3. Reheat over low heat on top of stove or in oven for 15 minutes. Turn into serving dish.

# *Haupia*
## *(Coconut Pudding . . . a traditional luau dessert)*

6 cups Coconut Cream
  (page 132 )
1 cup milk
1½ cups sugar
½ teaspoon salt

6 tablespoons cornstarch
  mixed with ¾ cup cold
  water
1 16-ounce can pineapple
  cubes

**DAY BEFORE PARTY:**
1. Combine Coconut Cream and milk and heat over low heat until just boiling. Add sugar, salt, and cornstarch-water mixture. Cook over medium heat, stirring constantly until pudding thickens. Pour into a greased mold and chill.

**AT SERVING TIME:**
1. Unmold Haupia. Serve on leaf-lined tray with pineapple cubes as garnish.

## *Pineapple Snow Pudding*

3½ cups pineapple juice
3 envelopes unflavored
  gelatin
6 tablespoons sugar
⅛ teaspoon salt
2 teaspoons grated
  lemon rind
¼ cup lemon juice

1½ cups heavy cream
1½ cups shredded coconut
4 cups halved fresh strawberries, mixed with 2 tablespoons sugar
4 canned pineapple slices,
  drained and quartered

**DAY BEFORE PARTY:**
1. In small bowl, stir gelatin and sugar into 1 cup pineapple juice. Let stand 5 minutes. Set bowl in boiling water; stir until gelatin is dissolved.
2. In large bowl, combine 2½ cups pineapple juice, salt, lemon rind, lemon juice, then stir in gelatin mixture. Refrigerate until mixture resembles unbeaten egg white.
3. With electric mixer at high speed, beat gelatin mixture until fluffy. Whip cream; quickly fold it and ¾ cup coconut into gelatin. Pour into 2 quart mold. Refrigerate until set.

**AT SERVING TIME:** Unmold pudding onto large dish; sprinkle top with coconut and some strawberries; arrange pineapple slices and remaining strawberries around base.

# *Daiquiri Chiffon Pie*

1 envelope unflavored gelatin
½ cup cold water
¼ teaspoon salt
5 eggs, separated
1 6-ounce can frozen
   daiquiri mix concentrate
2 or 3 drops green food color
   (optional)

½ cup sugar
½ cup heavy cream, whipped
1 baked 11-inch pie shell
1 cup whipped cream for
   garnish
fresh mint leaves for garnish

**EARLY ON DAY OF PARTY:**
1. Sprinkle gelatin on cold water in top part of a double boiler. Add the salt and egg yolks; mix well.
2. Place over boiling water and cook, stirring constantly, for 4 or 5 minutes, until mixture thickens slightly and gelatin is completely dissolved.
3. Remove from heat. Add the daiquiri concentrate and chill, stirring occasionally, until mixture mounds slightly when dropped from spoon. (Add food color if desired).
4. Beat egg whites until stiff but not dry. Gradually add sugar and beat until very stiff. Fold in the gelatin mixture; fold in the whipped cream. Turn into baked pie shell and chill until firm. Garnish at serving time with additional whipped cream and fresh mint.

# *Expenses for South Sea Islands Party for 20–25:*

$39.25    Rum Punch
2.30    Fruit Punch
9.10    Teriyaki on Skewers

| | |
|---:|---|
| 4.70 | Lomi Salmon |
| 11.15 | Islander Shrimp/Orange-Ginger Sauce |
| 3.70 | Rumaki |
| 1.50 | Macadamia Nuts |
| 12.75 | Roast Loin of Pork, Polynesian |
| 6.70 | Chicken Tahitian |
| 13.05 | Planked Fish baked in Coconut Sauce |
| 1.65 | Glazed Sweet Potatoes/Macadamia Nuts |
| 1.05 | Baked Bananas |
| 1.25 | Rice Papeete |
| .85 | Haupia |
| 2.75 | Pineapple Snow Pudding |
| 1.40 | Daiquiri Chiffon Pie |
| 3.00 | Fresh Fruit |
| $116.15 | |

Take 20 to 25 of your friends with·you on a trip to Polynesia; the "fare" is only about 4.60 a person.

# Buffets, Cocktail Parties, Special Occasions

## Skip a Birthday: Give a Greek Saint's Day Party for 30

Full scale birthday parties are usually the domain of little kids, septa-or-octogenarians ... or those special people like Queen Elizabeth and Elizabeth Taylor whose 40th birthday was cause for great whoop-de-do.

If you'd like to be sentimental on a grand scale for a husband, friend, or even (with appropriate lack of modesty) yourself, don't give a party on the celebrant's *birth*-day ... do up the occasion in festive style—à la grecque. Instead of honoring the day of birth, Greeks celebrate the Saint's Day for whom the person was named. There are dozens of saints on the Eastern Orthodox roster, all with a special day. For those whose names might be completely non-Greek (or who are named after more obscure, but nonetheless saintly, saints), they can celebrate on the grab-bag All Saint's Day, November 1.

In Greece (or among Greek-Americans) a Saint's Day party is always a very special occasion with traditional dishes, exhuberant music and dancing, and plenty of those very indigenous Greek beverages—ouzo, retsina, and metaxa brandy.

The most important Saint's Day on the Greek calendar is the Feast of St. Basil, whose birthday on January 1 provides an alternate way of celebrating New Year's Day. This is a family holiday where everyone sings "kalandas," traditional carols to St. Basil. A special cake (the "Vasilopeta") is blessed and baked with a coin in it, imparting extra good luck to the person who gets the piece with the coin. One of the best parties we ever went to was a Saint's Day party for a good friend, luckily named Basil. (Incidentally, a Bill can qualify as a Basil.) Although there were many Greek relatives and guests, perhaps a third of us were "outsiders." The food, drinks, and music were so elevating one couldn't help getting in the middle of a Kalamatianos dance to bound and bounce along with great enthusiasm, if not style.

The knack for socializing is something particularly Greek. It's interesting that in the language there is no word for "stand-offishness." The Greeks love to entertain—anybody! They are uninhibited and straightforward. In Greek the word "zenos" means *both* stranger and guest: all are treated the same.

The components for a smashing Saint's Day party are the same as they are for any party: good food, good drink, good music and, above all, a good mix of people. For a Saint's Day party, you must invite people who will turn on to the atmosphere and the music. Save the must-invite type of guest (your husband's boss?) for either a sedate dinner à quatre or for a broadside cocktail party where canapés and inspired martinis will make the party go.

For an invitation to a Saint's Day blast, your note might read:

**Andy and Nancy Day**
**invite you to celebrate**
**The Feast of St. Andrew**
**in authentic Greek style**
**on November 30th, at 8:00 p.m.**
**Don't bring gifts ... do bring a**
**wealth of energy and appetite**

As a guide to various name-day possibilities, here's a list of the leading Saint's Days in the Eastern Orthodox Calendar: *January:* 1, St. Basil the Great; 7, St. John the Baptist; 16, St. Anthony the Great; 25, St. Gregory the Theologian. *February:*

17, St. Theodore. *April:* 23, St. George; 25, St. Mark; *May:* 2, St. Athanasius; 8, St. John the Theologian; 21, St. Constantine and St. Helen; *June:* 12, Day of St. Peter and St. Paul; *July:* 20, Prophet Elias; 25, St. Anna; *September:* 16, Day of St. Euphemia; *October:* 18, St. Luke the Evangelist; 26, St. Demetrios; *November:* 14, St. Phillip; 25, St. Catherine; 30, St. Andrew; *December:* 4, St. Barbara; 6, St. Nicholas; 27, St. Stephen.

The food served at a Saint's Day party is richly traditional, since some authentic Greek recipes are more than 2,500 years old. The Greeks, a very inventive nation, devised the basic white sauce called Bechamel which is generally regarded as French. The Greeks did it first, however; the Italians borrowed the recipe, and the French took the credit! Greeks are also responsible for the basic brown sauce—Sauce Espagnole—a staple elegant French cooking. Incidentally, in Grecian cooking, the sauce is never something to be poured in a gravy boat or served on top of a dish—the sauce is always *integral* to the recipe, part of what makes the whole thing succeed, and is frequently cooked along with the dish. Our menu carries this out, including both white sauce (sometimes called "krema" or "saltsa besamel" in Greek cuisine) and the famous "avgolemeno" (egg and lemon sauce).

It was also Greeks who discovered how to fillet fish, use cabbage imaginatively, and create mountains of delectable pastry dishes, both entrées and desserts (with a little inspiration from the Turks).

Every book on Greek cooking will repeat the phrase "no Greek drinks without eating" which, you must agree, is a very sensible attitude. The Greeks get around it by enjoying "meze" (also called "mezethakia" or "orektika")—something to whet the appetite. Hence, Greeks vie very heavily with Scandinavians and Russians (who respectively have their smörgåsbord and zakuska) in setting forth a grand spread for what we call the cocktail hour.

In Greece, what to drink with meze is no great problem.

The national drink is "retsina" which shares popularity with the more familiar, anise-flavored "ouzo," similar to pernod. Ouzo, which turns white when diluted with water, actually means lion's milk—and you have to be lion-hearted to drink it for any kind of duration. Ouzo may be taken plain, with a little water, or on the rocks.

Retsina, on the other hand, is always served straight. This peasant favorite, incidentally, evolved from the days when Greek wines were stored in goatskins. The skins were smeared with pitch or resin to prevent leakage and spoilage, and the wine took on its characteristic resin taste. Even later, when earthenware jugs were used for storage, resin formed the seal for the pottery and the resulting resin-flavored wine became an acquired taste. In Greece, if you prefer to have plain wine you ask for it "aretsinoto" . . . but for your Saint's Day party, stay authentic with the real thing.

The menu would be considered splendid by the saints themselves with four savory, unusual meze; three main courses, two special vegetables plus salad and a cheese bread. The finale includes three succulent desserts, braced with good strong Kafes (Greek-Turkish coffee).

The counterpoint to the eating and drinking is, of course, the music and dancing. Many, many good bouzouki records are available from the library, all reflecting the popular music and dances which were done as far back as the days of Homer and Alexander the Great. While Greeks love to talk (they say conversation is more important than eating), they also love to sing and dance. In fact, in the country, peasants have a song for everything from sowing seeds to washing clothes.

Some of the more popular dances include the "Hassapiko" (butcher) for men only in which knives are wielded as the dancers whirl; the "Kalamatianos," done in a circle while a leader flaunting a handkerchief turns, twists, and jumps, and the remaining dancers shuffle along to a basic step; and the Cappadocian spoon dance in which participants hold pairs of

wooden spoons and beat out rhythm, similar to the way fla-
menco dancers use their castanets. In general, Greeks dance
to please themselves, and that's the attitude your guests
should have as they whirl, twirl, and get into the mood. (It
might be wise to eliminate the Hassapiko-knife-wielding
variation, however).

With enough merriment and good food, everyone, especially
the guest of honor, will adopt the marvelous Greek attitude
of "avrio" (tomorrow) which is roughly equivalent to the Spanish
"manana." At some point during the evening, proclaim a special
toast for the name-day-person: "Hronia Polla" (many years),
and then for all other drinking, the traditional term is
"Yásas!"—to your health.

Here's the elaborate, elegant, but largely do-ahead menu.
Authentically, it's not necessary in Greece to have hot food
absolutely hot or cold food completely cold, so serving on a
nicely set buffet will be adequate. You don't need sumptuous
chafing dishes to do the trick:

# Saint's Day Party for 30

## Meze (Appetizers)

Kavouri Mezethaki
(Crab Meat Canapes)

Tiropetes
(Cheese Puffs)

Keftedakia
(Cocktail Meatballs)

Taramosalata
(Red Caviar Dip)

## Entrade (Main Courses)

Moussaka
(Baked Eggplant and Meat Casserole)

Garides Tourkalimano
(Braised Shrimp and Rice)

Dolmadakia Me Avgolemono
(Stuffed Vine Leaves with Egg-Lemon Sauce)

Yemistes Domates Laderes
(Stuffed Tomatoes)

Spanokopeta
(Spinach Pie)

Salata Horiatiki
(Rural Salad)

Tiropsomo
(Cheese Bread)

## Glyka (Desserts)

Baklava
(Honey-nut Pastries)

Tourta Me Amygthala
(Almond-custard Torte)

Kourabiedes
(Greek Shortbread)

Kafes (Greek Coffee)          Metaxa Brandy

Ouzo and Retsina before and during dinner

# Kavouri Mezethaki
## (Crabmeat Canapés)

½ cup onions, chopped
1 stick butter
3 tablespoons flour
3 cups lukewarm milk
¾ cup breadcrumbs
1 teaspoon dried mint
1 teaspoon dried basil
Dash of pepper sauce
2 pounds crab meat

2 hard-boiled eggs, chopped
1 cup chopped mushrooms
2 tablespoons chopped
   stuffed olives
1 tablespoon sherry
Salt to taste
¾ cup melted butter
½ pound phyllo sheets

**ONE WEEK BEFORE PARTY:**
1. Sauté onions in butter in a large skillet. Stir in flour. Slowly add milk and blend until well mixed. Remove from heat. Add remaining ingredients except for phyllo sheets and melted butter, and mix well.
2. Brush one sheet of phyllo with melted butter. Place another sheet on top and butter. Divide crab meat filling into 5 portions. Place 1 portion 1″ from bottom and sides of longest edge and all the way across the phyllo.
3. Carefully roll as a jelly roll, folding side edges as you go along. Set roll on a cookie sheet. Repeat procedure with remaining 4 portions of crab meat, remembering to butter each sheet of phyllo before using. Cover rolls with plastic wrap and then tin foil and freeze.

**AT PARTY TIME:**
1. Preheat oven to 350°.
2. Bake frozen Kavouri Mezethaki on greased cookie sheets until golden, about 25 minutes. Slice in 1-inch pieces before serving.

# *Tiropetes*
## *(Cheese Puffs)*

2 pounds feta cheese
24 ounces cottage cheese
10 eggs

1 cup parsley, finely chopped
1 pound butter
2 pounds phyllo pastry sheets

### ONE WEEK BEFORE PARTY:
1.  Crumble feta into small pieces. Add cottage cheese and blend well. Add eggs and beat thoroughly. Add parsley.
2.,Melt butter. Carefully cut phyllo sheets into 3 equal portions (about 6″ × 9″ each; cut through several layers at once). Refrigerate ⅔ of sheets until needed and cover remaining third with a slightly damp towel.
3.  Remove one sheet of phyllo pastry, place on flat surface and brush with melted butter. Fold in long sides toward middle, making a strip about 2″ wide; butter again.
4.  Place 1 tablespoon of cheese filling near top in center, then fold over right corner of strip to meet left edge of strip, forming a triangle. Fold this triangle over and down again toward right side to form another triangle. Repeat left-to-right, right-to-left folding process until entire strip has been folded over and over into one plump triangle. Tuck edge underneath or inside. Brush top with butter.
5.  Place completed tiropetes on cookie sheets. When all are prepared, wrap in plastic, then foil, and freeze.

### AT PARTY TIME:
1.  Preheat oven to 350°.
2.  Bake frozen tiropetes on greased cookie sheets about 25–30 minutes or until puffed and golden.

# *Keftedakia*
## *(Meatballs Flavored with Ouzo and Mint)*

4 slices white bread, crusts removed, torn into small pieces.
¼ cup ouzo
¾ cup olive oil
1 cup finely chopped onions
1 pound lean ground lamb
1 pound lean ground beef
2 eggs

2 tablespoons finely cut fresh mint or 2 teaspoons dried mint
1 teaspoon minced garlic
1 teaspoon oregano
2 teaspoons salt
Freshly ground black pepper to taste
2 cups flour

**DAY BEFORE PARTY:**

1. Soak bread in ouzo for 10 minutes.
2. Meanwhile in large, heavy skillet, heat 6 tablespoons of olive oil over moderate heat. Add the onions and sauté, stirring frequently, for 5 minutes until onions are soft and transparent, but not brown. With slotted spoon, transfer onions to large mixing bowl. Set skillet aside, off heat.
3. Squeeze bread dry and discard ouzo. Add bread, ground meats, eggs, mint, garlic, oregano, salt and pepper to onions. Knead vigorously with both hands, then beat with wooden spoon until mixture is smooth and fluffy. Taste for seasoning.
4. Moistening hands periodically with cold water, shape meat mixture into balls about 1″ in diameter. Then roll balls in flour to coat them lightly, and refrigerate for about 1 hour.
5. Add remaining olive oil to oil in skillet and heat. When sizzling, drop 20 or 25 meatballs into hot oil and cook for 8 to 10 minutes, shaking pan from time to time to roll balls about and brown them evenly. Drain on paper towels. When all meatballs are brown (about 60), store in ovenproof serving dish or pie pan, cover and refrigerate overnight.

**AT PARTY TIME:**

1. Remove Keftedakia from refrigerator 1 hour before serving.
2. Heat in 350° oven for 5–10 minutes (not more!).

# Taramosalata
## (Red Caviar Dip–"Caviar of Athens")

**EARLY ON DAY OF PARTY:**
1. In blender container place juice of 2 lemons, an 8-ounce jar of red caviar, 1 average-sized onion (cut in ½″ pieces). Blend 1 minute, until smooth.
2. Remove crusts from 8 slices white bread and crumble. Dip bread into luke-warm water and squeeze dry. Add to blender and blend for about 30 seconds at low speed.
3. Remove lid and while blender is running at low speed, pour in 1 cup of olive oil. Blend until oil disappears. Refrigerate.

**AT PARTY TIME:**
1. Serve in a shallow, chilled bowl. Garnish with greek olives and serve with small chunks of Greek or Italian bread.

# Moussaka
## (Eggplant–Meat Casserole)

3 large eggplants
2 quarts water
½ cup salt
Flour for dredging
1 cup olive oil (hot)
6 tablespoons butter
3 cups finely chopped onion
2 cloves garlic, minced
1½ pounds ground round steak
1½ pounds lean ground lamb
2 cups canned tomato sauce
2 bay leaves
1 teaspoon oregano
Salt and freshly ground black pepper to taste
2 cups white wine
½ teaspoon cinnamon
2 tablespoons chopped parsley
10 fresh mushrooms
2 quarts Bechamel Sauce (below)
1 cup freshly grated Parmesan cheese

**DAY BEFORE PARTY:**
1. Preheat oven to 400°.
2. Cut eggplant into ¼″ thick round slices and cover slices with water and salt. Let stand 20 minutes; then drain. Rinse slices under cold water and dry on paper towels. Dredge eggplant in flour and brown quickly on both sides in hot oil. Drain on paper towels.
3. Heat 4 tablespoons butter in skillet and cook onion and garlic until golden. Add ground meats and cook about 10 minutes, stirring occasionally. Break up any lumps that form. Add tomato sauce, bay leaves, oregano, salt, pepper, wine, cinnamon, and parsley and blend well. Cook until almost all liquid is absorbed.
4. Wash and trim mushrooms and slice them. In a small saucepan or skillet sauté in remaining 2 tablespoons butter until golden brown. Add to meat.
5. Grease a 12″ × 16″ × 2″ roasting pan or baking dish and arrange half the eggplant slices on bottom. Add chopped meat mixture and cover with remaining eggplant slices.
6. Make Bechamel Sauce:

| | |
|---|---|
| 4 tablespoons butter | Salt and white pepper to |
| ¼ cup flour | taste |
| 5 cups milk | 4 egg yolks |
| | 1 cup heavy cream |

Melt butter in saucepan and blend in flour with wire whisk. Heat milk almost to boiling, then add all at once to butter-flour mixture, stirring vigorously with wire whisk. When mixture comes to boil it will automatically thicken. Let simmer 5 or 10 minutes more. Add salt and pepper.

Beat egg yolks lightly and blend with cream. Add a little of hot sauce to egg yolk mixture and return this mixture to sauce. Stir rapidly; adjust seasoning. Let cool for 10 minutes before adding to moussaka.
7. Pour cooled Bechamel Sauce over eggplant casserole and sprinkle with Parmesan cheese. Bake about 1 hour, or until top is golden. Refrigerate overnight.

**AT PARTY TIME:**

1. Remove Moussaka from refrigerator 2 hours before serving.
2. Preheat oven to 350°.
3. Reheat casserole for 15 minutes. Let stand about 15 minutes before serving.

# Garides Tourkalimano
## (Braised Shrimp with Rice)

1 cup chopped onion
3 cloves garlic, finely minced
½ cup olive oil
½ stick butter
1 cup dry vermouth
3 cups Italian-style stewed
  tomatoes
A pinch of rosemary

2 bay leaves
2 cups raw rice (one 16-ounce
  box
6 pounds jumbo shrimp,
  shelled and deveined
3 tablespoons chopped
  parsley
1 cup feta cheese, crumbled

**EARLY ON DAY OF PARTY:**

1. In large saucepan or a casserole that can be used over direct heat, sauté onion and garlic in oil and butter until onion is tender but not brown. (About 5 minutes).
2. Add wine, tomatoes, rosemary and bay leaves to onions and simmer, covered, 30 minutes. Remove bay leaves. Set sauce aside at room temperature.

**AT PARTY TIME:**

1. 30 minutes before serving, cook rice: Bring 4¾ cups of water with 2 teaspoons salt to a boil; add 2 cups rice; cover tightly, reduce heat and cook 25 minutes or until all water is absorbed.
2. Meanwhile, gently reheat sauce for 10 minutes. The add raw shrimp, parsley and cheese, cover pan and cook over medium heat for 10 minutes or until shrimp are tender. (*Don't overcook*). Serve with cooked rice.

# Dolmadakia Me Avgolemeno
## (Vine Leaves with Egg-Lemon Sauce)

1 pound vine leaves, bottled
   in brine
1½ pounds ground lamb
1 cup raw rice
1 small onion, minced
2 teaspoons oregano
½ teaspoon cinnamon
1 teaspoon salt
½ teaspoon black pepper

½ cup water
4 teaspoons olive oil
4 cups chicken bouillon or
   6 chicken bouillon cubes
   dissolved in 4 cups
   boiling water
2 tablespoons butter
4 eggs
6 tablespoons lemon juice

**EARLY ON DAY OF PARTY:**
1. Rinse each leaf one by one and cover with cold water while preparing filling.
2. Combine ground meat, rice, onion, oregano, cinnamon, salt, pepper, water and 2 teaspoons of olive oil.
3. Form meat mixture into small oblong mounds and place each on a vine leaf near the base. Fold the leaf over once, fold in edges, and roll up tightly toward point of leaf.
4. Pour remaining 2 teaspoons olive oil into large heavy saucepan or skillet with tight fitting lid. Line bottom with any leftover or torn vine leaves. Arrange Dolmadakia in pan close together (in layers if necessary). Pour 2½ cups of broth (reserve the rest) over Dolmadakia. Dot with butter. Cover with heavy plate to prevent stuffed leaves from opening as rice swells. Cover pan and simmer over low heat 45 minutes or until rice is tender. Set aside at room temperature.

**AT PARTY TIME:**
1. 15 minutes before serving, gently reheat Dolmadakia.
2. 10 minutes before serving, heat remaining 1½ cups bouillon in a small saucepan.

151

3. Meanwhile, in a bowl, beat eggs with lemon juice. Add ½ cup of hot bouillon, beating vigorously with wire whisk. Pour egg-lemon mixture into remaining broth, again beating energetically. When the sauce is completely blended, remove Dolmadakia from heat and pour sauce over it. Let stand for 5 minutes. Sauce will thicken. Serve quickly. (Makes 50–60).
NOTE: Dolmadakia Me Avgolemono should not be reheated as the sauce will curdle. If you must re-heat, warm very, very slowly in an uncovered pan.

## *Yemistes Domates Laderes*
### *(Stuffed Tomatoes)*

30 under-ripe tomatoes
  not too large
Salt to taste
Pepper to taste
Pinch of sugar
6 onions, finely
  minced
3 cups olive oil

⅔ cup parsley, chopped
½ cup chopped fresh dill or
  2 teaspoons dry dill
1 cup raisins
1 cup pignolia nuts
3 cups cooked rice
1 cup water

**DAY BEFORE PARTY:**
1. Wash tomatoes. Slice top off each and reserve. Scoop out pulp. Sprinkle inside of tomatoes with salt, pepper and sugar.
2. Sauté onions in ½ cup of olive oil until soft. Mix onions with parsley, dill, raisins, pignolia nuts, rice and 2 cups of olive oil. Season to taste with salt and pepper.
3. Fill tomatoes with this mixture. Cover with tomato caps and place in casserole with remaining ½ cup olive oil and 1 cup water. Weigh down tomatoes with heavy plate. Cover casserole and bake in preheated 350° oven for 30 minutes. Gently remove tomatoes to serving dish. Discard oil-water mixture. Cool to room temperature and refrigerate. Serve cold.

# *Spanakopeta*
## *(Spinach Pie)*

7 10-ounce packages of chopped, frozen spinach
4 tablespoons butter
4 tablespoons flour
2 cups milk
Salt and freshly ground pepper to taste
Dash of nutmeg
2 onions, chopped
1 stick butter

10 eggs, beaten
2 cups feta cheese, crumbled
½ cup parsley, minced
¼ cup fresh mint, minced, or
  1 tablespoon dried mint
Salt and pepper to taste
1 pound phyllo pastry sheets
2 cups melted butter
  (1 pound)
2 rectangular baking dishes,
  about 11" × 14" × 2"

**ONE WEEK BEFORE PARTY:**
1. Defrost frozen spinach and drain. Dry as thoroughly as possible on paper towels.
2. Make Bechamel Sauce: Melt 4 tablespoons butter in saucepan without letting it brown. Add flour and stir with whisk
until well blended. Meanwhile, bring milk almost to boiling
point, stir butter-flour vigorously and add hot milk all at once.
When mixture comes to boil it will automatically thicken. Simmer for 5 more minutes. Season to taste with salt, pepper and
dash of nutmeg. Cool.
3. In large skillet, sauté onion in butter until soft; add spinach
and saute 3 or 4 more minutes. Cool.
4. Turn spinach into large bowl; add cream sauce, eggs, cheese,
parsley, mint, and salt and pepper. Mix well. Test for seasoning.
5. Working with 1 baking dish at a time, brush 1 phyllo sheet
with butter, place in baking dish; repeat with 6 more phyllo
sheets, brushing each well with butter. Cover remaining phyllo
sheets with damp cloth to keep them moist. Add half of spinach

mixture to baking dish, spread out evenly, then place 7 or 8 more layers of phyllo sheets on top, buttering each sheet first. Repeat process with second baking dish. Cover with foil and freeze.

**AT PARTY TIME:**
1. Remove Spanakopeta from freezer 1 hour before serving.
2. Preheat oven to 350°; bake Spanakopeta for about 30 minutes or until crust is puffed and golden. Cut into small squares before serving.

## *Salata Horiatiki*
## *(Rural Salad)*

**NIGHT BEFORE PARTY:**
1. Rub a large wooden salad bowl with one clove of garlic. (If you're not using a wooden bowl, add minced garlic to dressing, instead.)
2. In a glass jar combine the following for salad dressing:

| | |
|---|---|
| 2 cups olive oil | 1 tablespoon salt |
| ⅓ cup lemon juice | 1 teaspoon freshly ground |
| ⅓ cup wine vinegar | pepper |
| | 1 tablespoon oregano |

Shake well and store at room temperature overnight.

**EARLY ON DAY OF PARTY:**
1. In prepared salad bowl or large serving bowl, combine:

| | |
|---|---|
| 1 head lettuce, torn into bite-size pieces | 4 cucumbers, peeled and sliced |
| 1 pound of chicory, torn into bite-size pieces | 2 green peppers, seeded and sliced in rings |

1 pound of romaine lettuce,
  torn into bite-size pieces
4 ripe tomatoes, cut into
  small wedges
1 package radishes, sliced

2 Bermuda onions, thinly
  sliced
2 tablespoons chopped
  parsley

2. Refrigerate until half an hour before serving.

**AT SERVING TIME:**
1. To salad vegetables add ½ pound feta cheese, crumbled;
½ cup black Greek olives, drained; ½ cup green olives, drained;
1 small can anchovies (drained and chopped), and 2 tablespoons
fresh mint (or 1 tablespoon dried mint).
2. Toss salad with prepared dressing. Adjust seasoning.

# *Tiropsomo*
## *(Cheese Bread)*

*Bread:*
1½ cups scalded milk
3 tablespoons sugar
3 teaspoons salt
⅓ cup shortening
1½ cups lukewarm water
3 packages yeast
10½ cups sifted flour
¼ cup melted butter or
  salad oil

*Filling:*
3 cups finely chopped parsley
2 garlic cloves, minced
2 tablespoons butter
3 eggs, lightly beaten
1½ pounds feta cheese,
  crumbled
freshly ground black pepper
  to taste
*Topping:*
2 eggs, beaten
¼ cup sesame seeds

## DAY BEFORE PARTY:

1. Add sugar, salt, and shortening to scalded milk. Stir; cool until lukewarm.

2. Pour water into large bowl, add the yeast. Stir until completely dissolved. Add the cool milk mixture.

3. Stir in 6 cups of flour and beat well. Then add the remaining flour, stirring until moistened. Let stand 10 minutes.

4. Turn dough out onto a floured surface and knead until smooth, about 10–12 minutes. Place in a large greased bowl, grease surface with melted butter or salad oil, cover, and let rise in warm place (80° to 85°) until dough doubles in bulk (about 45 minutes).

5. Punch dough down, turn out on a smooth surface, and let rest 10 minutes.

6. Grease 3 9"×5"×3" bread pans.

7. Make Filling:

A. Cook parsley and garlic in butter over moderate heat, stirring until parsley is wilted but not browned. Cool.

B. Add all but 3 tablespoons of beaten eggs (reserve for Step 9, below) to parsley-garlic mixture. Fold in crumbled cheese and black pepper.

8. Divide dough in thirds and shape each third into a ball. Roll each ball into a rectangle about ¼" thick and about 10" wide.

9. Brush with lightly beaten egg reserved from filling and spread filling over dough to about 1" from edges. Roll in jelly-roll fashion and pinch edges to seal. Place in prepared pans with seam side down. Let rise in a warm place until higher in middle than edge of pans, about 1 hour.

10. Brush with beaten eggs. Sprinkle with sesame seeds and bake in 400° preheated oven until golden brown, about 55 minutes. Cool to room temperature and wrap in foil. Refrigerate.

## AT PARTY TIME:

1. preheat oven to 350°. Slice bread in ½" pieces. Heat foil-wrapped bread for about 10 minutes.

# *Baklava*
## *(Honey-nut Pastries)*

1½ pounds ground walnuts
1 pound ground almonds
1 teaspoon cinnamon
½ teaspoon ground cloves

¾ pound sweet butter,
  melted
1 pound phyllo pastry sheets
Syrup (below)

**DAY BEFORE PARTY:**
1. Mix together walnuts, almonds, cinnamon and cloves.
2. Butter 16½″ × 11″ baking pan and fit 6 or 7 pastry sheets on bottom, brushing each one first with melted butter.
3. Sprinkle with one-quarter of nut mixture. Add 5 or 6 more phyllo sheets, buttering each one, then another quarter of the nuts. Continue this procedure until all nuts are used, ending with 8 to 10 individually buttered pastry sheets as top layer.
4. With sharp knife, mark in diamond pattern; don't cut all the way through. Bake at 325° for 1½ hours.
5. Make Syrup:

1 cup honey
2 cups water
Juice of half a lemon
½ lemon, sliced thin

½ orange, sliced thin
1½ cups sugar
1 cinnamon stick

Combine all ingredients. Bring to boil and simmer 20 to 25 minutes. (If using candy thermometer simmer until syrup reaches 225°.) Strain, cool, and pour over hot baklava. Cover baklava with plastic wrap and store overnight at room temperature.

**AT PARTY TIME:**
1. Cut through baklava diamonds and serve in individual portions.

# *Tourta Me Amygthala*
## *(Almond Torte)*

9 eggs, separated
1 cup granulated sugar
¼ teaspoon cinnamon
1 cup plus 1 tablespoon
  breadcrumbs

Juice and chopped rind of
  ½ orange
1¼ cup chopped almonds
1 ounce unsweetened
  chocolate, grated

**EARLY ON DAY OF PARTY:**

1. Beat egg whites until foamy; add sugar gradually and continue beating until stiff. Fold in beaten egg yolks, cinnamon, 1 cup breadcrumbs, orange juice and rind, almonds and chocolate. Fold just until well blended.

2. Grease a 10″ spring form pan and sprinkle with 1 tablespoon breadcrumbs.

3. Pour mixture into pan and bake at 325° for 1 hour. Remove from oven and cool.

4. When cake has cooled for 1 hour, prepare custard:

2 eggs, separated
2 sticks sweet butter,
  softened

1 cup strong coffee,
  room temperature
4 cups powdered sugar
1 cup almonds, toasted
  and chopped

Beat egg yolks; blend in butter and coffee and add the sugar gradually until custard is thick. Beat 2 reserved egg whites until stiff and fold into custard mixture.

5. Assemble cake: Remove sides and bottom of pan. With a sharp, serrated knife, slice torte in half. Spread ¼ of custard on 1 layer. Place second layer on top of first. Spread remaining custard on top and sides of cake. Sprinkle top and sides with toasted, chopped almonds.

# Kourabiedes
## (Greek Shortbread)

1 cup walnuts or almonds
1 pound sweet butter at
  room temperature
¾ cup confectioners sugar
1 egg yolk

1½ tablespoons brandy
4 cups all-purpose flour
1 teaspoon baking powder
Confectioners sugar for
  topping

**TWO OR THREE DAYS BEFORE PARTY:**
1. Place nuts in blender container. Grind coarsely.
2. Cream butter until very light, using an electric mixer. Add sugar and beat until mixture is fluffy and pale in color.
3. Beat in egg yolk, brandy, and nuts.
4. Sift flour and baking powder together. Blend into butter mixture.
5. Shape into small balls (about ¾" in diameter) with floured hands. Bake in preheated 425° oven for 15 to 20 minutes or until very lightly browned. They should be pale in color.
6. Cool cookies slightly, then transfer to piece of waxed paper coated with sifted confectioners sugar. Sift additional sugar over top of warm cookies. (About 10 dozen small cookies.) If you can find the miniature paper cups used for petit fours, this is an attractive way of serving Kourabiedes).

# Kafes
## (Greek Coffee)

**AT PARTY TIME: *For 40 Demitasse Cups***
½ pound Greek or Turkish coffee
½ cup sugar
5 quarts of water.

1. Place coffee and sugar in a large coffee-pot, or use 2 12-cup coffeepots. Add water and stir until water, coffee and sugar are well mixed. Heat and wait until coffee comes to boil.

2. As soon as coffee reaches boil, remove pot from heat and pour a little coffee into each cup to be served. (This is called the "kaïmak"—the cream—of the coffee.) Return pot to heat and allow coffee to boil up again. Pour a little more coffee in each cup. Repeat procedure once more, then fill cups. The grounds are served in the cup with coffee so each guest should let his coffee stand a few seconds before sipping to allow grounds to settle.

## *Expenses for a Greek Saint's Day Party for 30:*

| | |
|---|---|
| $ 13.50 | Ouzo (2 fifth's) |
| 9.80 | Retsina (4 quarts) |
| 10.25 | Kavouri Mezethaki (crabmeat canapes) |
| 11.60 | Tiropetes (cheese puffs) |
| 3.80 | Keftedakia (cocktail meatballs) |
| 7.00 | Taramosalata (red caviar dip) |
| 9.90 | Moussaka (eggplant and meat casserole) |
| 25.30 | Garides Tourkalimano (braised shrimp and rice) |
| 4.75 | Dolmadakia Me Avgolemono (stuffed vine leaves) |
| 5.05 | Yemistes Domates Laderes (stuffed tomatoes) |
| 6.50 | Spanokopeta (spinach pie) |
| 6.65 | Salata Horiatiki (rural salad) |
| 6.45 | Tiropsomo (cheese bread) |
| 5.75 | Baklava (honey nut pastries) |
| 3.35 | Tourta Me Amygthala (almond torte) |
| 1.85 | Kourabiedes (Greek shortbread) |
| 2.00 | Kafes (Greek coffee) |
| 12.00 | Metaxa brandy |
| $145.50 | |

Your Greek Saint's Day party for 30 guests will cost under $5.00 a person.

**DAY BEFORE PARTY:**
1. Prick eggplant with fork and bake on cookie sheet in 350°
oven until tender.
2. Mince onions, tomatoes, and garlic. When eggplant is soft,
peel and remove seeds. Chop pulp and combine with onions,
tomatoes, and garlic. Blend in olive oil and salt and pepper
to taste. Turn into serving bowl and refrigerate overnight.

**AT PARTY TIME:**
1. Serve cold accompanied by party rye or pumpernickel.

# *Loukom Ikra*
## *(Mushroom Caviar)*

1 medium-sized onion,
  minced
2 tablespoons olive oil
½ pound mushrooms,
  chopped
1 tablespoon lemon juice

Salt and pepper to taste
1 tablespoon chopped chives
1 tablespoon sour cream
1 loaf party rye or pumpernickel

**DAY BEFORE PARTY:**
1. Sauté onion in hot olive oil until tender. Add mushrooms
and cook until brown. Add lemon juice, salt and pepper. Stir
in chopped chives and sour cream. Refrigerate overnight.

**AT PARTY TIME:**
1. Serve cold with slices of party rye or pumpernickel bread.

# Agurkai Su Rukscia Grietne
## (Cucumber and Sour Cream Salad)

**Salad:**
8 cucumbers peeled, halved,
   seeded and cut in ¼" slices
2 tablespoons kosher salt
1 teaspoon white vinegar

**Dressing:**
6 hard-boiled eggs
2 teaspoons prepared
   mustard
⅔ cup sour cream
¼ cup white wine vinegar
½ teaspoon sugar
White pepper to taste
   lettuce leaves and fresh
   (or dried) dill for garnish

**DAY BEFORE PARTY:**

1. Combine cucumber slices, salt and vinegar in mixing bowl; toss lightly until cucumber is moistened. Marinate at room temperature for about an hour. Then drain cucumbers; pat dry with paper towels.

2. Cut hard-boiled eggs in half; scoop out yolks and puree through a strainer, using the back of a spoon. Add mustard, sour cream, vinegar, sugar, and pepper.

3. Cut egg whites into narrow strips and add to a large bowl along with cucumbers. Pour egg yolk mixture over cucumbers-egg whites and blend gently. Adjust seasoning. Cover with plastic wrap and refrigerate.

**AT PARTY TIME:**

1. Serve cold on bed of lettuce with dill sprinkled on top of salad.

# *Salat*
## *(Vegetable Salad)*

1 cup vegetable oil
1 cup white vinegar
1 teaspoon salt
½ teaspoon white pepper
1 cup cooked green beans,
  cut in 1″ pieces
1 cup fresh cooked carrots,
  diced
½ cup raw celery, diced
1 raw cucumber, cubed
1 small onion, chopped
1 cup cooked green peas

1 cup cold, cooked potatoes,
  cubed
½ cup canned diced beets
1 cup pickled cauliflowerets
2 sour pickles, cubed
4 chopped anchovy fillets
1½ cups mayonnaise
  or more
1 cup mayonnaise to coat
  salad
Capers, pimiento, black
  olives for garnish

**DAY BEFORE PARTY:**
1. Mix oil and vinegar, salt and pepper together in a glass jar.
Shake well.
2. Marinate all the vegetables (except beets and pickled
cauliflower) with oil-vinegar mixture. Reserve a little of the
marinade and in a separate bowl add it to the beets. After an
hour or two, drain the vegetables well; pat dry with paper towels.
3. In a large bowl, gently combine all vegetables. Mix with
pickles, anchovies, and mayonnaise. Taste for seasoning; if
necessary add more salt, pepper, and mayonnaise. Cover with
plastic wrap and refrigerate overnight.

**AT PARTY TIME:**
1. Pile salad high on an attractive platter. If you can make it
stand in a pyramid shape it will be an appealing addition to
your zakuska table. Cover with a smooth thin layer of mayonnaise. Garnish with capers, pimiento strips and black olives.

# *Bliny*
# *(Buckwheat Pancakes)*

**Batter:**

| | |
|---|---|
| 1 cup lukewarm water | 1 teaspoon salt |
| 3 packages active dry yeast | 2 teaspoons sugar |
| 1 cup buckwheat flour | 6 tablespoons melted butter |
| 4 cups white flour | 6 tablespoons sour cream |
| 4 cups lukewarm milk | 6 egg whites |
| ½ cup melted butter | 6 egg yolks, beaten |

**TO PREPARE BLINY:** You can make all the bliny a week before the party, freeze them and then reheat at party time, or make them just before the guests arrive and keep warm until serving; or you may want to make a ceremony out of the actual cooking and prepare each blin to order at the table. In any case, remember to allow six hours from the start of the batter to bliny-making time!

1. Pour lukewarm water into small bowl and sprinkle in yeast. Let stand 2 or 3 minutes, then stir to dissolve. Place in warm, draft free spot for 5 minutes or until mixture almost doubles.

2. In large bowl, combine ½ cup of buckwheat flour and the 4 cups of white flour. Make a well in the center and pour in 2 cups of lukewarm milk and the yeast mixture. With mixer at low speed, blend flour and liquid ingredients; then at medium speed beat for several minutes until mixture is smooth. Cover bowl loosely with a dish towel and set aside in draft free spot for 3 *hours*, or until doubled in volume.

3. With a wooden spoon, stir batter thoroughly and beat in remaining ½ cup of buckwheat flour. Re-cover and let batter rest in warm draft-free spot for 2 *more hours*.

4. Again, stir batter vigorously and beat in remaining 2 cups of lukewarm milk, 6 egg yolks, salt, sugar, butter and sour cream.

5. In a separate bowl, beat egg whites until stiff; then, using

174

a rubber spatula, fold whites gently into bliny batter. Cover with a towel and let batter rest once more in its favorite spot for *30 minutes.*

6. Heat griddle until a spot of water races across it (or temperature of 375°). Pour 2 tablespoons of batter (1 full plastic coffee measure is a convenient dipper) for each blin. Coat top lightly with melted butter, then turn and cook another minute or so until golden.

**TO KEEP WARM UNTIL SERVING:**
Stack completed bliny in a baking dish. Cover with foil and keep at room temperature until 15 minutes before serving. Warm in 200° oven. Bliny can be served plain with just butter and sour cream, or with caviar, salmon, or mushroom and onion filling.

**TO FREEZE:**
Cut off about 1 yard of aluminum foil; center a piece of cardboard (a shirt stiffener works fine) and make piles of the cooked bliny, stacking about 5 or 6 bliny to a pile. Let cool to room temperature. Cover with foil and freeze. AT PARTY TIME: remove bliny from refrigerator 1 hour before serving. Reheat in 250° oven for about 15 minutes or until heated through. (Remove the cardboard first!)

*Fillings For Bliny:*

| | |
|---|---|
| 1 cup melted butter | 1 pound thinly sliced smoked |
| 3 cups sour cream | salmon, cut in small pieces |
| 8 ounces red caviar | to match size of bliny |
| 7 ounces black caviar (or more | Mushroom and onion filling |
| depending on your budget) | (see below) |

# *Griby S Loukom*
## *Mushroom-Onion Filling*

| | |
|---|---|
| ½ pound fresh mushrooms | Dash of nutmeg |
| 2 tablespoons butter | 1 teaspoon lemon juice |

½ cup chopped onion
½ teaspoon salt
Freshly ground pepper

2 teaspoons flour
½ cup sour cream
1 teaspoon dried dill

**SEVERAL HOURS BEFORE SERVING:**
1. Trim off tough stems of mushrooms and wipe with damp paper towels. Chop fine.
2. Heat butter, add mushrooms and onion and cook briskly for about 4 minutes, stirring occasionally.
3. Sprinkle with salt, pepper, nutmeg, lemon juice and flour. Cook 2 minutes longer. Remove from heat, blend in sour cream and dill. Store at room temperature for several hours before using. May also be served cold.

## *Expenses for Maslinitsa Feast for 20:*

| | |
|---|---|
| $16.00 | Russian Vodka (2 fifths) |
| 1.25 | Bitki (beef balls) |
| 2.35 | Pozharsky (veal balls) |
| 1.80 | Pirozhki (cabbage-carrot filling) |
| 3.90 | Pirozhki (salmon filling) |
| 3.45 | Dragomirovsky Vorschmack (this and that casserole) |
| .60 | Loukom Ikra (mushroom caviar) |
| 1.45 | Baklazhannaia Ikra (eggplant caviar) |
| 2.05 | Agurkai su Rukscia Greitne (cucumbers in sour cream) |
| 2.95 | Salat (vegetable salad) |
| 2.50 | Bliny |
| .75 | Smetana (sour cream) |
| .40 | Maslo (melted butter) |
| 8.00 | Ikra: red caviar (8 ounces) |
| 30.00 | Ikra: black caviar (7 ounces, average between $15.00 to $50.00 for 7 ounces) |

| | |
|---|---|
| 6.00 | Lososina (smoked salmon) (1 pound) |
| .70 | Griby S Loukom (mushroom and onion filling) |
| 2.00 | Bliny with currant jam and sour cream |
| .75 | Coffee |
| $84.90 | |

$4.25 a person will provide a lavish Maslinitsa bliny party for 20 guests.

# Ole: Mexican Three Kings' Day Party for 8 Adults and 8 Children

Christmas-time all over the world is the season for party-going and giving and general merrymaking. The quality of the fun usually has little to do with the quantity of money available. Happily, more often than not, the Christmas spirit really does prevail.

One country where this is especially true is Mexico where the predominantly Roman Catholic population begins festive celebrating on December 16th. For the next 22 days, special foods are prepared, songs sung, gifts exchanged, and posadas (parties) enjoyed. The season ends on January 6th with Dia de Los Reyes—Kings' Day—corresponding to our Twelfth Night.

The unusual Kings' Day traditions provide ideal inspiration for an American version that includes children as well as their parents. Often, a party is either geared for the kids or the grown-ups but rarely both. Dia de Los Reyes, however, is one such happy marriage of both generations.

A buffet of special holiday foods may vary from one posada to the next, but the desserts served on Kings' Day are almost rigid and universal: Rosca de Los Reyes (Kings' Day Bread), and Buñuelos, fried, sweet puffs, dipped in honey or sugar.

Aside from being a delicious dessert-bread, Rosca de Los Reyes has some delicious traditions going for it. When the bread is prepared a little china doll or large lima bean is baked right in. Whoever finds the doll or the bean in his piece of bread is king or queen for the night. But there's another tradition as well: whoever gets the doll or bean must give the next party, traditionally on February 2, Candlemas Day. It used to be a custom to swallow the "prize," so make sure the doll called for in our version is big enough to be noticed.

The buñuelos also have their own holiday ritual . . . one which I'm not too sure you'll want to follow. In the province of Oaxaca, people save their cracked or imperfect pottery for the entire year and then during the Christmas festivities, eat buñuelos served in a cracked plate. When the puff is finished they throw away the dish! This goes on for each buñuelo eaten—and the amounts eaten are prodigious. It may be more propitious to savor the puffs and forget the custom.

Your own Christmas decorations will serve as appropriate background, but you might give the table a little more atmosphere with an informal setting incorporating some Mexican accents. Check the import shops to see if you can find a group of the tiny figures so popular for Mexican creches; use them for a timely and unusual centerpiece.

Another decor focal point, displayed in a prominent place, and incidentally, not within easy reach of breakables, will be the piñata: the pièce de resistance of the children's day. If you're really industrious you can make up your own piñata with papier mache . . . or buy a big clay olla (pot) in an import store. Fill the olla or your own version with small unbreakable gifts (2 or 3 little toys for each of the children, plus holiday wrapped candies). Then cover and decorate it with colored tissue paper to resemble an animal, boat, flower, clown or whatever strikes your fancy. The piñata should be strung on a rope attached to the ceiling (or a lighting fixture), but another length of rope should hang free so the piñata can be manipulated out of reach by the children while one blindfolded child tries to hit the piñata with a stick.

You might want to have one special gift for the piñata wrecker ... but of course, all the other goodies are jointly shared. Trading off should provide another 15 minutes worth of party-activity!

The first part of the evening should be devoted to eating—a universally acceptable format, right? After dinner it's time for dancing and the ritual of the piñata.

Adults can manage the buffet rather easily (with a little help from some snack tables), but it's difficult for children to juggle silver, dishes, and the rest. Why not set up a special and vividly decorated table for them—even in the kitchen—so they can enjoy their feasting in one safe, non-tippable spot?

A good time to schedule the party would be about 4:00 on a Sunday afternoon nearest the January 6th Feast Day. Don't plan on too long a cocktail hour—children get restive—and regarding adults, you don't want tequila in its various guises to take any glory away from the authentic array of food that's waiting to be savored.

Incidentally, tequila has been a mexican "bebida" (drink) for over 200 years and it's named for the town of Tequila which first started brewing it. Contrary to popular belief, tequila doesn't come from a cactus, but from an agave plant. The classic way of drinking tequila is to take a lick of salt, a sip of tequila and a suck of lime. Your male guests will all delight in showing how proficient they are at this machismo routine. The ladies will undoubtedly be quite happy with Margaritas and Tequila Sunrises.

Here's the menu for a Dia de Los Reyes feast that everyone will enjoy:

# Mexican Three Kings' Day Party for 8 Adults and 8 Children

Tequila          Margaritas          Tequila Sunrise

Tepache (Pineapple Punch)


## Appetizers

Guacamole with Tostada Chips
(Avocado Dip)

Bolas De Queso
(Chili Cheese Balls)


## Main Course

Enchiladas De Polo
(Chicken Enchiladas)

Enchiladas De Res Enrolladas
(Beef Enchiladas)

Chiles Rellenos Con Queso
(Stuffed Peppers with Cheese)

Berenjiena À La Acapulco
(Eggplant, Acapulco Style)

Calabazas Rellenos
(Stuffed Zucchini)

Frijoles Refritos
(Refried Beans)


## Desserts

Buñuelos
(Fried Sweet Puffs)

Rosca De Los Reyes
(Three Kings Bread)

Fresh Fruit

Sangria

Cerveza (Beer)

Cafe

Chocolate

# *Margarita Cocktails*

**SEVERAL HOURS BEFORE PARTY TIME:**
IN A GLASS BOTTLE, combine
   Juice of 4 limes (reserve 2 or 3 lime shells)
   ½ cup Triple Sec
   1 cup Tequila
Cover, shake well and refrigerate. (Makes 6–8 Margaritas.)

**AT PARTY TIME:**
1. Rub rim of cocktail glass with lime half; dip rim in saucer of salt. Fill with Margarita mix.

# *Tequila Sunrise Cocktails*

**SEVERAL HOURS BEFORE PARTY TIME:**
In a glass bottle, combine:
   Juice of 4 limes
   2 tablespoons Grenadine
   2 teaspoons Creme de Cassis
   1 cup Tequila
Cover, shake well and refrigerate. (Makes 6–8 Tequila Sunrises.)

**AT PARTY TIME:**
1. Add ice to large old-fashioned glasses; fill two-thirds with Tequila Sunrise mix; splash with club soda and garnish with a slice of lime.

# *Tepache*
## *(Pineapple Punch)*

| | |
|---|---|
| 2 large cans pineapple juice | 1 can pineapple cubes, |
| 1 quart club soda or ginger ale | drained |
| | Maraschino cherries |

**SEVERAL HOURS BEFORE SERVING:**
1. Combine pineapple juice and club soda or ginger ale. Refrigerate.
2. On thin plastic straws or toothpicks, spear a pineapple cube and a cherry; make about 16 or 20 spears. Cover with plastic wrap; set aside.

**AT PARTY TIME:**
1. Serve punch with or without ice, garnished, with a pineapple-cherry spear.

# Guacamole
## (Avocado Dip)

2 large ripe avocados
3 tablespoons lemon juice
1 small onion, chopped
1 small green chili, chopped
⅛ teaspoon coriander
Salt to taste
½ clove garlic, minced

3 tablespoons mayonnaise
1 ripe tomato, peeled, seeded
  and chopped
1 teaspoon Worcestershire
  sauce
Dash of cayenne pepper
Tostada chips

**EARLY ON DAY OF PARTY:**
1. Peel avocados and remove the seeds, but don't discard them. Mash pulp with a fork.
2. Add remaining ingredients (except tostada chips). (If you prefer smoother guacamole, run entire mixture briefly through blender—about 10 seconds). To keep mixture from discoloring place avocado seeds in the purée. Cover with plastic wrap. Refrigerate.

**AT SERVING TIME:**
1. Remove seeds from guacamole. Serve in a bowl on platter surrounded by tostada chips.

# Bolas De Queso
## (Chili Cheese Balls)

3 tablespoons jalapeno
   chilies, chopped
½ pound grated Parmesan
   cheese

½ pound cream cheese
2 egg yolks
1 cup breadcrumbs
Fat for deep frying

**DAY BEFORE PARTY:**
1. Clean jalapenos well, removing oil and seeds. Chop.
2. Mix cheese, cream cheese and egg yolks together until smooth. Form into 1″ balls. Roll in bread crumbs. Refrigerate 1 hour.
3. Heat oil. Deep fry balls, a few at a time until golden brown. Drain on paper towels. Place in a pie tin or baking dish. Cover with aluminum foil. Refrigerate overnight.

**AT PARTY TIME:**
1. Remove from refrigerator 1 hour before serving.
2. Re-heat in 250° oven for 10–15 minutes.

# Enchiladas De Pollo
## (Chicken Enchiladas)

5 cups diced, cooked chicken
¾ pounds grated cheddar
   cheese

1 pint sour cream
16 tortillas
Fat for frying

**EARLY ON DAY OF PARTY:**
1. Combine chicken meat, grated cheese and sour cream.
2. Fry tortillas in deep fat, one at a time until soft, then dip in chili sauce mixture. (See recipe below)

3. Fill tortillas with chicken mixture and roll. Place rolls close together in a flat, greased casserole; cover with plastic wrap and refrigerate.

**AT PARTY TIME:**
1. Remove from refrigerator 1 hour before serving.
2. Preheat oven to 350°.
3. Pour about 1½ cups of remaining chili sauce over enchiladas. Bake until thoroughly heated (about 15 minutes).

## *Chili-Tomato Sauce*

(This recipe makes enough sauce for use in Chicken Enchiladas, above, and Beef Enchiladas, following)

2 medium onions, minced
2 tablespoons salad oil
2 #2½ cans (7 cups) of tomato
  purée
4 cloves garlic, minced

3 tablespoons chili powder
  or more, to taste
1 teaspoon cumin
½ teaspoon oregano
2 teaspoons salt

**EARLY ON DAY OF PARTY:**
1. Sauté onion in oil until golden and tender.
2. Add tomato purée and garlic. Gradually stir in chili powder. Add cumin, oregano, salt. Adjust taste. (It should be quite "hot.") Cover and simmer 30–40 minutes, stirring frequently.
3. Let cool to room temperature. Put through blender for 30 seconds. Use part of the sauce in the two enchilada recipes; reheat remaining sauce to serve at the buffet.

# Enchiladas De Res Enrolladas
## (Rolled Beef Enchiladas)

**Ground Beef Filling:**
1 pound lean ground beef
1 or 2 tablespoons salad oil
1 medium sized onion,
  chopped
½ cup Chili Tomato Sauce
  (page 185)

**Enchiladas:**
½ cup vegetable oil for frying
  tortillas
¾ cup chopped onion
2½ cups Chili Tomato Sauce
  (page 185)
1½ cups grated sharp cheddar
  cheese

1. Make beef filling: In frying pan, brown beef in oil; add onion and cook until soft, moisten with sauce. Simmer slowly for 10 minutes.
2. Meanwhile, in a large frying pan, fry tortillas in oil until just soft, then dip in chili sauce.
3. Spoon about 3 tablespoons ground beef filling down center of each tortilla; sprinkle with 2 teaspoons onion. Roll tortilla around filling, and place seam down in shallow, greased casserole, enchiladas close together. Cover with plastic wrap and refrigerate.

**AT PARTY TIME:**
1. Remove from refrigerator about 1 hour before serving.
2. Preheat oven to 350°.
3. Pour about 1½ cups of chili sauce over enchiladas. Sprinkle with shredded cheese. Bake until thoroughly heated (about 15 or 20 minutes). Serve with remaining 1 cup of sauce. Optional: you may also serve with 2 cups of chilled sour cream on the side.

# For Pancake Lovers: Russian
# Maslenitsa (Pre-Lent) Party for 20

An attempt to condense Russian cuisine in a few brief pages is about as futile as explaining how the telephone works to a 4-year-old child. (Actually, I can't explain it to *anyone,* so the analogy is even more apt.)

The term Russian cooking is in itself a misnomer, because Russia is only one of 15 republics in the U.S.S.R. Russia is the largest, and therefore represents many different customs, languages, and varieties of cooking. To boggle the mind even further, in the U.S.S.R. there are 110 different national strains . . . and a dozen different climates . . . and over 250 million people.

So until we write an entire cookbook on the U.S.S.R., which would be quite a job (and also a jeopardy—I'm sure it would involve the addition of at least 25 pounds to my already threatened waistline), we'll restrict our discussion to Russia alone . . . and, in fact, to several specific traditions that can be adapted into an unusual and barrier-breaking American party.

The broad tradition takes in a holiday called Maslenitsa, a week-long "butter festival" featuring bliny (buckwheat pancakes) that precedes the 40 days of lent. Maslenitsa is similar to Mardi Gras and Shrove Tuesday festivals which have one last blast of celebrating before the sober, fasting period of Lent begins. But Maslenitsa is more than a religious festival. In certain areas of the U.S.S.R. the celebration of Maslenitsa is also an ode to the arrival of spring and departure of winter.

The butter used to coat the pancakes is supposed to represent the sun, the onset of spring. Participants offer "Knlib i sil" (bread and salt) as a guesture of showing winter out and welcoming springtime in. Winter also receives a pitcher of wine as a going away present and all the guests drink toasts to the departure.

Two important customs are mandatory with the celebration of Maslenitsa: partaking of "zakuska" (small bites) a custom observed in all houses, however poor, as a way of welcoming a hungry guest, no matter what the season; the second custom is the sharing of buckwheat bliny, pancakes about 3″ or 4″″ across, embellished with various fillings.

About the zakuska: in the country, the custom is so accepted that in days past (and possibly even now in some remote areas) a zakuska table, even though very modest, was kept stocked all day long because people might arrive at any time, and this was a way to satisfy them until dinner could be prepared. How much more gracious than the usual American procedure of dragging out some cheddar cheese, saltines and potato chips!

In the most aristocratic houses (before the Communist system abolished the theory of such a class-dominated society), the zakuska table might hold as many as a hundred different dishes, hot and cold, spicy and bland—caviar, herring, salmon, fish, eggs, salads, patés, vegetables, aspics and little savory pies. And every dish, like the Swedish smörgåsbord, would be a picture for the eye, garnished with capers, olives, hard-boiled eggs, dill, slices of tomato. Then and now, it's not enough to put out a lavish spread for your household—it should be a feast for the eye as well as the palate.

Each zakuska should be washed down with a little glass of chilled vodka, taken all in one gulp. Today, Russian homes may have only two or three zakuska before dinner, but the vodka custom is still observed to get the appetite going.

While caviar was and is part of a respectable zakuska table, for our purposes and economies we have included it in the second part of a Maslenitsa feast: the bliny buffet. Russians have been eating bliny in one form or another for over 1,000 years. In the country the dish can be provincial food; in the cities it becomes ultimately sophisticated. The distinction depends on the topping or the stuffing. Melted butter and sour cream are, of course, crucial no matter what the filling, since the dairy orgy is part of the last gasp before lenten fasting.

Bliny are not just your ordinary pancake. Sure—they're in the same family with griddle cakes and, more elegantly, crepes, and someplace in the middle, tortillas, manicotti, and the Scandinavian plätter. But a good bliny batter is a six-hour project: not that you have to actually work that long, but it takes that much time for the yeast to rise and the sour cream to work, but more about that later.

If you want to schedule a pre-lent party and call it a Maslenitsa—this is it. Or, opt for an event as a way of welcoming spring (this year's alternate to Walpurgis night in Sweden, see page 195), but in any case, it will be a delightful culinary treat for your guests.

Crucial to the celebration is a good stock of Russian vodka. In America, vodka is often used in "non-offensive" drinks: a vodka and tonic ... or a Bloody Mary ... or the vodka martini for the executive who doesn't want his boss to know he drinks at lunch. But in Russia, there are dozens of varieties of vodka and they bear little resemblance to the mixed-beverages we're used to. Good Russian vodka is rather smooth and tastes more like whisky or even brandy.

Originally introduced as a medicine in the 14th century (like the Dutch Genever gin), vodka in Russia has become a drink that *accompanies* food—not simply a pre-dinner cocktail. And vodka goes with any food except the sweetest course. By the time you serve dessert, no one will want to drink anything else anyway—except coffee!

If you can get Zubrovka (a vodka with a blade of buffalo grass in it for flavor) you'll be really treating your guests. If you can't, serve ice cold 80-proof vodka (leave the 100 proof for summer vodka-and-tonics, or for really intrepid drinkers).

The Russians would never spoil good vodka by putting it on the rocks, so for your party, chill the vodka and have a cache of shot glasses; then be stingy with the size of the shots.

The idea is that for each bite of zakuska... or bliny... one takes a small glass of vodka. (Interestingly, in some areas of the U.S.S.R., men finish off their zakuska or bliny with a glass of ale, very similar in custom to the Swedish way of drinking aquavit with beer.)

For a Maslenitsa party, your centerpiece could be a big bowl of fruit, very traditional at Russian gatherings... along with a big, fat loaf of brown Russian-type bread (Jewish rye or pumpernickel will do) and a bowl of rough salt for the "knlib i sil". (For those who want to follow the custom, the idea is to cut a slice of bread, dip it in the salt and eat, the meaning being that even if our house is so poor we only have bread and salt, we are willing to share!)

For a spring-welcoming, joyous accent, get some authentic balalaika music... or if you're dealing with a more elegant group, play some of the great Russian classics: Rachmaninoff, Tschaikowsky, Borodin (on whose music the lovely *Kismet* is based). One of the best parties we ever had included a marvelous Russian emigré who got in the mood to sing... and did so... à capella... for 40 minutes or so until we finally had to call a halt and get on with the bliny.

It's only outside of Russia that the delicate fish eggs are called "caviar" from the Turkish word "khavyah." The Russians refer to caviar in all its many grades as "ikra." You can have the finest black or gray ikra... or stay with the tasty but less budget-wrecking red caviar for your party. Caviar for a Maslenitsa party goes with the bliny, along with a smear of melted butter and a topping of sour cream: delightful!

Here's the menu for a Maslenitsa party. It should be a ball, and if anyone gets grumpy you can always banish them (for pretend, of course) as the Ghost of Winter. The happiest, verviest of the ladies should undeniably be named Spring! As they say in old Russia: "Na zdorovie!"—to your health!

# Russian Maslenitsa (Pre-Lent) Party for 20

### Russian Vodka

### Zakuska
### (Appetizers—Small Bites)

Bitki
(Beef-balls)

Pozharsky
(Veal Balls)

Pirozhki
(Cabbage-Carrot Filling)

Pirozhki
(Salmon Filling)

Dragomirovsky Vorschmack
(This and That Casserole)

Loukom Ikra
(Mushroom Caviar)

Baklazhannaia Ikra
(Eggplant Caviar)

Agurkai Su Rukscia Grietne
(Cucumber in Sour Cream Sauce)

Salat
(Vegetable Salad)

### Bliny
### (Buckwheat Crepes)

*served with:*

Smetana (Sour Cream)

Maslo (Melted Butter)

Ikra (Red and Black Caviar)

Lososina
(Smoked Salmon)

Griby S Loukom
(Mushroom and Onion Filling)

### Slatkoye
### (Dessert)

Bliny with Black Currant Jam and Sour Cream

### Coffee

# Bitki and Pozharsky
## (Cocktail Meatballs)

Bitki and pozharsky are all relatives of croquettes, quenelle, fricadelle, and godiveaux. Bitki are beefballs; pozharsky are made of chicken or veal.

## Bitki

3 slices white bread with crusts removed, coarsely diced
½ cup milk
1 pound ground chuck, ground twice
1 minced onion
1 egg
1 teaspoon salt
½ teaspoon peper
1 tablespoon parsley
3 tablespoons sour cream
3 tablespoons corn oil
3 tablespoons butter
¾ cup plain bread crumbs

**DAY BEFORE PARTY:**
1. Soak bread in milk for a few minutes; then wring out and shred bread.
2. In mixing bowl, shape hollow in center of meat. Add bread, onion, egg, salt, pepper, parsley and sour cream. Mix thoroughly until blended.
3. Roll meat mixture into walnut-size balls (about 1″). Quickly roll in breadcrumbs. Chill for 1 hour.
4. Heat oil and butter. Sauté meat balls until brown on all sides; about 15 minutes. Drain on paper towels. (Reserve oil for Pozharsky.)
5. Store Bitki in pie tin or other baking dish; cover and refrigerate overnight.

# *Pozharsky*
## *(Chicken or Veal Balls)*

Follow recipe for Bitki, substituting 1 pound of ground veal or chicken for ground chuck.

### AT PARTY TIME:
1. Remove Bitki and Pozharsky from refrigerator 1 hour before serving.
2. Preheat oven to 350°. Reheat Bitki and Pozharsky for 10 minutes. Serve with toothpicks.

# *Pirozhki*
## *(Little Pies)*

### TWO DAYS BEFORE PARTY:

### *MAKE DOUGH:*

1½ cups butter, room temperature
1½ 8-ounce packages cream cheese (12 ounces, total), room temperature
½ teaspoon salt

3 cups unsifted flour
1 egg yolk, beaten with 2 teaspoons milk or cream

1. Beat butter, cream cheese and salt together with mixer until smooth and well blended. With beater at low speed, blend in flour until particles are pea-sized. Turn into plastic bag and knead until smooth dough forms. Flatten dough into an 8" or 10" square. Cover with plastic wrap. Chill overnight.

**DAY BEFORE PARTY:**

*MAKE FILLINGS:*

### Cabbage-Carrot Filling

2 cups chopped white
cabbage
1 tablespoon salt
1 onion, chopped
¼ cup butter

2 large carrots, cubed (½")
1 tablespoon chopped
parsley
2 hard-boiled eggs, chopped
Salt and freshly ground
pepper to taste

1. Mix cabbage with salt; let stand 15 minutes. Squeeze out water. Blanch cabbage in colander over steam for 5 minutes. Drain.
2. Sauté onion in butter. Add cabbage and carrots and cook slowly for half an hour. Add parsley and eggs; season with salt and pepper. Cool.

### Salmon Filling

¼ cup onions, chopped
½ garlic clove, minced
¼ pound mushrooms,
chopped
1 tablespoon fresh dill
or 1 teaspoon dried dill
¼ cup dry vermouth
1 teaspoon salt

Freshly ground black pepper
Dash nutmeg
1 7-ounce can salmon,
drained and flaked
1 cup cold cooked rice
1 teaspoon lemon juice
1 hard-boiled egg, chopped

1. Sauté onions and garlic in butter until tender. Add mushrooms and dill and cook for 3 to 5 minutes.

2. Add vermouth, salt, pepper and nutmeg and bring mixture to a boil. Consistency should be thick. If there is too much liquid, evaporate by additional cooking; if too dry, add a little more wine.

3. Mix mushroom mixture with salmon and rice; add lemon juice and chopped eggs.

**DAY BEFORE PARTY:**
*TO ASSEMBLE PIROZHKI:*

1. When fillings are ready, remove dough from refrigerator about 5 minutes before rolling. Divide dough in half for Cabbage-Carrot filling; return other half to refrigerator. Roll dough on floured pastry cloth with floured rolling pin ... or roll between two sheets of waxed or plastic paper. Roll out to a rectangle about 12″ × 18″. Cut in 3″ rounds.

2. Center 1 teaspoon of filling on each round; moisten edges of pastry with pastry brush dipped in water and fold together over filling. Lay on side and press edge with floured tines of fork to seal.

3. Set pastries seam side up on ungreased cookie sheet. Flatten slightly and pinch ends to give traditional oval shape with pointed ends. Chill 1 hour. Repeat with remaining dough and salmon filling.

4. Brush with beaten egg yolk. Bake in moderate oven, 350°, 25 to 30 minutes until golden.

**AT PARTY TIME:**

1. Remove Pirozhki from refrigerator about 1 hour before serving.

2. Preheat oven to 350°. Heat Pirozhki for 5 to 10 minutes so that they are heated through.

# Dragomirovsky Vorschmack
## (This and That Casserole)

¼ cup minced onion
2 tablespoons butter
1 cup chopped mushrooms
1 cup diced leftover beef
1 cup diced ham
1 cup diced cooked chicken
1 cup diced boiled potatoes
1 dill pickle, diced

½ cup olives, stoned, diced,
  green or black
Salt to taste
Pepper to taste
1½ cups sour cream
2 hard-boiled eggs, chopped
2 or 3 tomatoes, sliced
Grated cheese

**DAY BEFORE PARTY:**
1. Sauté onion in butter. Add mushrooms and cook until tender. Combine with beef, ham, chicken, potatoes, dill pickle and olives. Add salt and pepper to taste. Mix with sour cream.
2. Turn mixture into buttered baking dish and cover with hard-boiled eggs. Surround with tomato slices. Sprinkle grated cheese over top and bake in moderate 350° oven until thoroughly heated and brown.
3. Cool to room temperature. Cover and refrigerate overnight.
**AT PARTY TIME:**
1. Remove casserole from refrigerator about 1 hour before serving.
2. Preheat oven to 350°. Reheat for 15 minutes until warmed through.

# Baklazhannaia Ikra
## (Eggplant Caviar—Poor Man's Caviar)

1 large eggplant
2 onions
4 skinned, seeded tomatoes

4 cloves garlic
¾ cup olive oil
Salt and pepper to taste
party rye or pumpernickel

# Chiles Rellenos Con Queso
## (Stuffed Peppers with Cheese)

*Salsa de Jitomate:*
3 tablespoons chopped onion
1 garlic clove, minced
1 tablespoon butter
1 16-ounce can Spanish style
   tomato sauce
⅓ cup water
¼ teaspoon salt
½ teaspoon oregano

1 can (7 ounce) California
   green chiles
½ pound jack cheese
½ cup flour
3 eggs
3 tablespoons flour
¼ teaspoon salt
Vegetable oil for frying

**EARLY ON DAY OF PARTY:**

1. Make Salsa de Jitomate (Tomato sauce); Sauté chopped onion and garlic in butter until golden. Stir in tomato sauce, water, salt, and oregano. Simmer 15 minutes. Set aside until serving time.

2. Drain canned chiles, rinse and cut a slit down the side of each. Remove seeds and pith. Cut jack cheese into pieces about ½" wide, ½" thick and 1" shorter than the chiles. Stuff each pepper. Roll stuffed chiles in ½ cup flour to coat all over; gently shake off excess.

3. Separate eggs, beat whites until they form soft peaks. Beat yolks with 1 tablespoon water, 3 tablespoons flour and ¼ teaspoon salt until thick and creamy. Fold into whites.

4. Heat oil to depth of about 1" in a wide frying pan over medium heat. Dip stuffed chiles into egg batter, place on a saucer and slide into hot oil. When bottoms are golden, turn gently with spatula and cook other side. (About 3 minutes per side). Drain on paper towels. Turn into oven-proof casserole or baking dish. Cover and store at room temperature.

**AT PARTY TIME:**

1. Re-heat chiles rellenos in 200° oven for 10–15 minutes.

2. Re-heat Salsa de Jitomate for 10 or 15 minutes or until bubbling hot.

# Berenjiena À La Acapulco
## (Acapulco Style Eggplant)

1 large eggplant
Boiling salted water
½ cup bread crumbs
½ cup grated Parmesan
   cheese

¼ cup butter
Salt and pepper to taste
½ pound fresh mushrooms,
   sliced
1 16-ounce can tomato sauce

**DAY BEFORE PARTY:**
1. Place whole, unpeeled eggplant in boiling, salted water to cover completely; reduce heat. Simmer for 10 minutes. Drain and cool.
2. Cut eggplant into quarters lengthwise; peel each quarter, then cut crosswise, into 1-inch pieces.
3. Mix bread crumbs with grated cheese.
4. In a buttered 2-quart casserole, arrange a layer of eggplant pieces, dots of butter, a sprinkling of salt and pepper, sliced mushrooms, tomato sauce and the crumb-cheese mixture, *USING HALF OF ALL INGREDIENTS.* Repeat layers once more.
5. Bake casserole uncovered in 350° oven for 25 minutes. Cool to room temperature and refrigerate.

**AT PARTY TIME:**
1. Remove from refrigerator about 1 hour before serving.
2. Heat in 350° oven until bubbling (about 10–15 minutes).

# Calabazas Rellenos
## (Stuffed Zucchini)

6 medium-sized zucchini
1 3-ounce package cream
   cheese

1 teaspoon salt
1 teaspoon pepper

2 tablespoons minced onion

1 cup sour cream
Paprika

**DAY BEFORE PARTY:**
1. Place whole unpeeled zucchini in boiling water to cover. Reduce heat and simmer uncovered until nearly tender—about 10 minutes. Remove from water and cool.
2. Cut each zucchini in half lengthwise and remove pulp and seeds. Mix pulp and seeds with cream cheese, onion, salt and pepper.
3. Stuff mixture back into zucchini shells; arrange on a buttered baking dish. Refrigerate overnight.

**AT PARTY TIME:**
1. Remove from refrigerator about 1 hour before serving.
2. Spoon sour cream over each zucchini. Sprinkle with paprika. Bake 10 minutes in 350° oven.

## *Frijoles Refritos*
## *(Refried Beans)*

2 pounds dried pinto or
  pink beans, cleaned
  and rinsed
2 or 3 medium onions,
  minced

10 cups water
¾ cup hot bacon drippings
  or lard
Salt to taste

**DAY BEFORE PARTY:**
1. Combine beans in pan with onions and water. Bring to boil. Cover and remove from heat for 2 hours.
2. Return to heat, bring to boil and simmer slowly until beans are tender, about 3 hours. Mash bean-onion mixture with potato

ricer and add bacon drippings or lard. Mix well.
3. Continue cooking, stirring frequently until beans are thick and fat is absorbed. Season to taste. Turn into baking dish or serving casserole. Cover and refrigerate overnight.

**AT PARTY TIME:**
1. Remove casserole from refrigerator about 1 hour before serving.
2. Reheat gently for 10 minutes in 350° oven.

# *Buñuelos*

1 13¾ ounce package of hot roll mix (with yeast)
1 egg
2 cups corn oil for deep frying
Glazed and sugar coatings (below)

**EARLY ON DAY OF PARTY:**
1. Pour ¾ cup warm water into bowl. Sprinkle in yeast and stir until dissolved.
2. Add 1 egg; stir in flour from package. Blend. Cover and let rise in warm place until doubled in size, about 40 minutes.
3. Shape the dough in walnut-sized balls. Place on a tray, and let rise another 30 minutes.
4. Heat oil in deep fryer. When temperature reaches 375°, add one or two buñuelos to the fryer at a time. Turn once; remove when golden. Drain on paper towels. Repeat procedure until all puffs are cooked.

*FOR GLAZE:*
1. Place ½ cup granulated sugar, ½ cup light brown sugar, and ½ cup water in frying pan. Add 1 tablespoon butter, 1 teaspoon cinnamon, and 1 tablespoon dark corn syrup. Heat, stirring until sugar melts. Then boil for 1 or 2 minutes, until 2 drops of syrup run together off spoon.

2. Remove from heat. Cool for 1 minute. Place half of the buñuelos in pan, one at a time, and spoon syrup over puffs until coated on both sides. Drain on a wire rack for 30 minutes.

**SUGAR COATING:**
1. In plastic bag, add 1 cup granulated sugar and 1 teaspoon cinnamon. Shake to mix. One at a time, add a warm buñuelo to bag and shake to coat.

**AT PARTY TIME:**
1. After cooking other dishes, place buñuelos in still-warm oven until ready to serve for dessert.

## *Rosca De Los Reyes*
## *(Three Kings Bread)*

2 packages yeast
1 cup warm water
5 cups unsifted all-purpose flour
¼ cup instant non-fat dry milk
1 cup soft butter
½ cup granulated sugar
1 teaspoon salt
3 eggs
Butter
½ cup raisins
½ cup chopped walnuts

¼ cup chopped candied cherries
1 tablespoon grated orange peel
1 tablespoon grated lemon peel
3 tablespoons heavy cream
2 cups confectioners sugar
½ teaspoon vanilla
Candied fruits and nuts for garnish
A little glass doll or lima bean for the "prize"

**DAY BEFORE PARTY:**
1. Dissolve yeast in warm water. Add 1¼ cups unsifted flour and dry milk; beat well with wooden spoon for several minutes.

Cover and leave in warm place about one-half hour.

2. In separate bowl, cream butter with sugar and salt. Beat in eggs, one at a time. Add to the yeast-flour mixture, beat for another 3 minutes. Gradually stir in remaining 3¾ cups unsifted flour.

3. Turn out dough on lightly floured board and knead until smooth and elastic (about 7 minutes). Place in a buttered bowl. Turn once to bring buttered side up; cover with a dish towel and allow to rise in warm place until almost doubled (about 1½ hours).

4. Combine raisins, walnuts, candied cherries, orange and lemon peel. Pat dough into 10" round on floured board. Top with fruit-nut mixture and roll up edges of dough. Knead until fruit and nuts are evenly distributed.

5. Divide dough in half. Form each half into a long roll; join ends of each roll to form rings and place each on a greased cookie sheet. Cover and allow to rise for about 30 minutes.

6. Preheat oven to 400°. Bake loaves for 25 to 30 minutes. Cool. Cut out small triangle from the top of one and insert doll or lima bean. Replace wedge.

7. Combine cream, powdered sugar, and vanilla; glaze loaves. Decorate with additional candied fruits and nuts in Christmas motif.

**AT PARTY TIME:**

If desired, place loaves in warm oven with Buñuelos until serving time.

# Orange Sangria

| | |
|---|---|
| 2 medium oranges | 2 bottles dry red wine |
| ½ cup confectioners' sugar | 1 cup Cointreau |
| 1 quart orange juice | |

**EARLY ON DAY OF PARTY:**
1. Cut oranges in half. Cut 3 or 4 thin slices from 1 half to be used later for garnish. Peel remaining halves. With spoon bruise peel with sugar to release oils.
2. In large jar or container, combine orange juice, wine, and liqueur. Add orange peel.
3. Cover and chill. (After 1 hour remove orange peel).

**AT PARTY TIME:**
1. Serve sangria with ice cubes. Cut orange slices into quarters or eighths to garnish each cup.

## Expenses for a Dia de Los Reyes Party for 8 Adults, 8 Children:

| | |
|---|---|
| $ 6.80 | Tequila |
| 4.80 | Margaritas |
| 4.60 | Tequila Sunrise |
| .95 | Tepache (punch) |
| 1.55 | Guacamole (avocado dip) |
| 1.85 | Bolas de Quesa (chili cheese balls) |
| 5.95 | Enchiladas de Pollo (chicken enchiladas) |
| 2.85 | Enchilades de Res Enrolladas (beef enchiladas) |
| 1.85 | Chiles Rellenos Con Queso (stuffed peppers with cheese) |
| 1.80 | Berenjiena à la Acapulco (eggplant Acapulco) |
| 1.05 | Calabazas Rellenos (stuffed zucchini) |
| .65 | Frijoles Refritos (refried beans) |
| 1.00 | Buñuelos (fried sweet puffs) |
| 2.70 | Rosca de Los Reyes (Three Kings Bread) |
| 3.00 | Fresh fruit |

```
   3.70    Sangria
   3.00    Cerveza (beer)
    .75    Cafe
    .75    Chocolate
 $45.60
```

$2.85 per person will cover 16 guests handsomely at your Three Kings' Day Party.

# Welcome Sweet Spring:
# Walpurgis Night Smorgasbord
## for 24–30

Spring comes a little later to Sweden than to most parts of the United States, but when it arrives our Scandinavian friends know how to celebrate! All over Sweden on April 30th, Walpurgis Night, the coming of Spring is observed with lit bonfires (and lit bonfire-lighters), all-night revelry, boistrous parties, smörgåsbord, and the mandatory and plentiful aquavit.

If you want to welcome Spring in authentic Swedish style, wait until April 30th or the closest convenient date ... or forget Spring and give a smörgåsbord buffet whenever you have the inclination, budget and, frankly, the energy to work up the lavish assortment of specialty dishes for a feast that approximates a traditional smörgåsbord. (You can only come fairly close because in fine Swedish restaurants the buffet usually includes a dozen or more dishes in any of several categories.

To begin with, you should understand the philosophy of a smörgåsbord which literally means "bread and butter" table and originally was *not* a complete meal. In Norway, smörgåsbord is called "koldtbord" (cold table) and in Denmark it's "smørrebrød (smeared bread).

If you're served smörgåsbord in a Swedish home it will be followed by a proper meal, a meat course plus vegetables, and then dessert. In a restaurant, smörgåsbord is usually *the meal*, followed by dessert and coffee.

An authentic "bread and butter" table cannot be described as a collection of haute cuisine food. The Swedes like simpler cooking with an emphasis on sea food, a natural since the country is bordered on east and south by the Baltic Sea and lakes cover about 9% of Sweden's area. So a smörgåsbord will include fish in several different guises; cold and hot, pickled or plain. The smörgåsbord always begins with herring, clearly the favorite fish in all Scandinavian countries. Some restaurants feature as many as 25 different herring dishes for this traditional first course.

For a smörgåsbord keep the decorating simple. The lavish array of food should prove the most important focal point. And in true Swedish fashion, each dish must be attractively presented and garnished with parsley, or slices of hard-boiled egg, radishes, or sprinkles of dill, etc.

Since each course deserves a clean dish, it will probably be necessary to either rent dinner plates or use paper plates of good, nonbendable material. Of course, china is nicest and the usual rates are about 10¢ a dish, so if you want to do the buffet properly, it's worth renting them.

The same is true with silver. While knives aren't necessary for our menu, it's awkward to ask guests to "keep your fork, please." Clearly, fresh forks with each course are a nice touch. Fortunately, forks don't have to match, and cake forks are suitable for the first and second courses, therefore, you may only have to rent 50 forks (about 10¢ each).

I'm recommending renting rather than borrowing silver and china from friends. One of your neighbor's plates is sure to be the one to break, and her precious silver fork is the one that will get mangled in the dishwasher or thrown out with the garbage.

Another important point: for a party this size, outside help can be a blessing. The serving takes care of itself but washing those 100 dishes and forks can be mind-boggling without a helping hand.

By now you probably have visions of dozens of used dishes and forks piled up near your once-attractive buffet. Eliminate this confusion by planting a tea-cart near the smörgåsbord table so guests can deposit the "empties" before going on to the next phase. It's easy enough for you (or your temporary maid) to wheel them into the kitchen, unload quickly, and station the cart once more near the smörgåsbord. This is infinitely better than having "helpful" guests run in and out of the kitchen, depositing used dishes in utter chaos.

You should arrange your buffet in traditional Scandinavian style with each course somewhat separated from the rest. And then be sure to guide guests on the proper procedure. This is the way it goes with our smörgåsbord:

# Walpurgis Night Smörgåsbord for 24–30

### 1. Herring dishes first:

Glasmästarsill
(Glassblower's Herring)

Sillisalaatti
(Herring in Sour Cream)

### 2. Other fish dishes and pickled salads

Varm Krabbsmörgås
(Crab Canapés)

Gravad Lax
(Marinated salmon)

Pressgurka
(Cucumber salad)

Lag Beta
(Pickled beets)

### 3. Cold meats and additional salads

Has-Notkott Platta
(Ham and Roast Beef Plate)

Lever Svenskt
(Swedish Liver Pâté)

Gurka Surgrädde
(Cucumbers in Sour Cream)

Potatissalad Med Ansjovis
(Potato Salad with Anchovies)

Lök Paj
(Onion Pie)

### 4. Hot dishes, called "Småvarmt" (small warm)

*Kaaldomer*
*(Stuffed Cabbage)*

*Små Köttbullar*
*(Swedish Meatballs)*

*Kalvrulader*
*(Veal Rolls)*

*Hasselbackpotatis*
*(Roasted Potatoes)*

*Bruna Bönor*
*(Brown Beans)*

If you have chafing dishes, this is the time to use them. Hot trays are risky because guests will be going all around the table and someone is sure to trip on a cord! Rent or borrow chafing dishes if you need them. Or keep the "småvarmt" course warm in the kitchen until you see guests are well into their third course of cold meats and salads.

5. Dessert and coffee are the last course and should be served from a separate area much, *much* later. Dessert is:

*Socker Strutar–*
*Sugar Cones with Whipped Cream and Lingonberries*

*Kaffe–Coffee*

Now that you know what and in which order to eat, let's talk about the drinking essential for Walpurgis Night, and certainly necessary for any successful party, smörgåsbord or no.

Scandinavians aren't really fond of cocktails. The preferred tradition is to precede food with aquavit—the water of life—except in Finland where vodka is the choice. Aquavit is chilled and taken straight or in a Swedish version of a boilermaker: aquavit plus beer. The practice is to then continue right on with aquavit and beer all through dinner. Generally, aquavit when chilled is almost tasteless, although some versions are spiced with herbs. In the U.S. for example, Danish Akvavit with caraway flavoring is often served. (In Norway, Sweden and Denmark there are more than 50 different types of aquavit.)

The aquavit, which reputedly aids the digestion, is supposed to create a "trou" (hole) in the stomach for the food eaten so you can put in more food. Then you have a sip of beer as a chaser. A word about beer. It has a much higher status in Sweden and Denmark than it does here. Scandinavians consider beer a fine drink to accompany their herring and it certainly goes well with salted fish and pickled salads.

# *Glasmästarsill*
## *(Glassblower's Herring)*

**Pickling Liquid:**
1½ cups white vinegar
1 cup water
1 cup granulated sugar

4 salted herring, about 3 pounds, cleaned, scraped and soaked in cold water for 12 hours OR 8 canned matjes herring fillets
3 small red onions, sliced
3 carrots, peeled and sliced
4 tablespoons horseradish
4 teaspoons allspice (whole)
4 teaspoons whole mustard seeds
5 bay leaves

**FOUR DAYS BEFORE PARTY:**
1. Bring vinegar, water and sugar to boil in a 3 quart stainless

steel saucepan, stirring until sugar completely dissolves. Cool to room temperature.

2. Meanwhile, wash herring and cut into 1″ pieces. Arrange a thin layer of onions in a 2-quart glass jar or two 1-quart glass jars. Top with a few slices of herring, carrots, and horseradish; sprinkle with allspice, mustard seeds and a bayleaf. Continue layering until all ingredients have been used.

3. Pour cooled pickling liquid into jar or jars. Cover securely and refrigerate for 4 days. Serve cold.

## *Sillisalaatti*
## *(Herring Salad in Sour Cream)*

(This dish, incidentally, is reputed to be a great morning after cure).

2 cups chopped herring
(matjes, pickled, or
Bismarck)
1 cup finely chopped cold
boiled potatoes
4 cups chopped cold cooked
beets (reserve juice for
sauce, below)

1 cup chopped apple
⅔ cup minced onion
¾ cup minced dill pickle
8 tablespoons chopped dill
4 tablespoons white wine
vinegar
Salt and pepper to taste

**DAY BEFORE PARTY:**

1. In large mixing bowl combine herring, potatoes, beets, apple, onion and pickle. Mix dill with vinegar and add salt and pepper. Pour over salad ingredients and toss gently.

2. Make Dressing:

6 chilled hard boiled eggs
2 tablespoons prepared
mustard

4 tablespoons white wine
vinegar
½ cup vegetable oil
6 tablespoons heavy cream

Remove yolks from eggs. Mince whites and set aside. Force yolks through sieve into small bowl, add mustard and mash to a paste.

Gradually beat in vinegar and oil, then cream (a tablespoon at a time) until sauce resembles heavy cream. Pour over salad. Mix lightly. Cover and chill overnight.

3. Make sauce: Stir 4 tablespoons reserved beet juice and 1 teaspoon lemon juice into 2 cups sour cream until smooth and well blended. Cover and refrigerate.

**AT PARTY TIME:**

1. Turn Sillisalaatti into attractive serving dish. Serve cold with sour cream-beet juice sauce on the side.

## *Varm Krabbsmörgås*
### *(Crabmeat Canapés)*

½ pound frozen crab meat, drained and cleaned
1 tablespoon dry sherry
1 teaspoon salt
¼ teaspoon white pepper
1 tablespoon chopped fresh dill

1 tablespoon butter
1 tablespoon flour
1 egg yolk
1 cup light cream
8 slices white bread

**EARLY ON PARTY DAY:**

1. In large mixing bowl combine crab meat, sherry, salt, pepper and dill. Set aside.

2. Melt butter without browning in a small heavy saucepan; remove from heat and stir in flour.

3. In small bowl, beat egg yolk with cream and stir this mixture into flour roux with wire whisk. Return pan to heat and cook slowly, whisking constantly for several minutes until mixture thickens. Don't let it boil!

4. Pour sauce over crab meat mixture in bowl and stir with a spoon until all ingredients are well mixed. Taste for seasoning.
5. Cut four rounds from each slice of bread, using small cookie cutter or glass. Toast bread on one side only under broiler. Set aside at room temperature. Refrigerate crab meat.

**AT PARTY TIME:**
1. Preheat broiler.
2. Spread untoasted side of prepared bread rounds with crab meat mixture, mounding up a little bit.
3. Place under broiler for 4 or 5 minutes before serving.

# *Gravad Lax*
## *(Grilled Marinated Salmon)*

This dish is often served raw, but to balance the uncooked glassblower's herring, we present it as served in many Scandinavian restaurants.

| | |
|---|---|
| 4 pounds raw salmon steaks, cut 1 inch thick | 15–20 sprigs fresh dill, chopped |
| ½ cup rough salt | 1 teaspoon white pepper |
| ¾ cup sugar | |

**TWO DAYS BEFORE PARTY:**
1. In a shallow bowl, cover salmon with salt, sugar, dill, and pepper, working well into the salmon. Let stand in refrigerator weighed down by a heavy plate for 2 days.

**AT PARTY TIME:**
1. Remove fish from refrigerator about 1 hour before serving.
2. Preheat broiler. Scrape seasonings from salmon. Grill 3 minutes on each side. The fish will be brown on the outside, still cold inside. Slice in 1″ portions on the diagonal, removing skin. Serve with Gravlaxsås (mustard sauce).

# Gravlaxsås
## (Mustard Sauce)

¾ cup Dijon mustard
2 teaspoons dry mustard
½ cup sugar

½ cup white vinegar
1 cup vegetable oil
½ cup fresh chopped dill

**DAY BEFORE PARTY:**
1. In small deep bowl, mix both mustards, sugar, and vinegar until it forms a paste. With wire whisk, slowly beat in oil until mixture is thick, like mayonnaise. Stir in chopped dill.
2. Refrigerate overnight, tightly covered.

**AT PARTY TIME:**
1. Shake vigorously or beat with whisk before serving.

# Pressgurka
## (Cucumber Salad)

5 large cucumbers
2 teaspoons salt
2 teaspoons sugar

½ cup vinegar
White pepper to taste
Chopped parsley (about ½ cup)

**DAY BEFORE PARTY:**
1. Peel cucumbers, leaving a little skin on for color. Halve cucumbers lengthwise and scoop out seeds. Slice thin and sprinkle with salt. Refrigerate for one hour; drain.

2. Sprinkle cucumbers with sugar and pour vinegar over them. Sprinkle with pepper and parsley. Serve cold.

## Lag Beta
### (Pickled Beets)

1 cup vinegar
1 teaspoon salt
1 minced garlic clove

½ cup brown sugar
2 teaspoons pickling spices
2 1-lb. cans sliced beets, drained

**DAY BEFORE PARTY:**
1. Combine vinegar, salt, garlic, sugar and spices in saucepan. Bring to boil, simmer for several minutes and pour over beets.
2. Cool to room temperature; then refrigerate overnight. Serve cold.

## Lever Svenskt
### (Swedish Liver Pâté)

1 pound calves liver
Milk
½ pound fresh pork fat
1 medium onion, coarsely chopped
5 anchovy fillets, chopped
2 eggs, separated

⅔ cup cream
1 teaspoon salt
½ teaspoon white pepper
Pinch of allspice
¼ teaspoon ginger
2 hard-boiled eggs, sieved

**DAY BEFORE PARTY:**
1. Wash liver. Soak in milk to cover several hours. Drain and wipe dry. Remove any membrane with a sharp knife. Cut liver

into small pieces. Add liver, pork fat, onions, and anchovies to blender container. Whirl until smooth.
2. Add egg yolks, cream and seasonings to mixture. Turn on blender and mix just until well combined.
3. Beat egg whites to soft peaks; fold pâté into whites.
4. Grease a 9" × 5" × 3" loaf pan. Line with brown paper, grease paper and pack in liver mixture. Cover with aluminum foil. Bake in a pan of hot water in a slow oven (300°) for 1 hour and 15 minutes. Cool to room temperature. Refrigerate overnight.

**AT PARTY TIME:**
1. Turn out on platter, remove paper, and garnish with sieved eggs. Serve with Swedish crackers or thin brown bread.

## *Gurka Surgrädde*
### *(Cucumbers in Sour Cream)*

4 large cucumbers, peeled and very thinly sliced
3 teaspoons salt
2 cups sour cream
4 tablespoons lemon juice
2 tablespoons minced onion
4 tablespoons chopped dill pickle

½ teaspoon sugar
1 teaspoon white pepper
6 radishes, thinly sliced
3 teaspoons chopped parsley
Lettuce leaves for garnish

**DAY BEFORE PARTY:**
1. Toss cucumbers lightly with 2 teaspoons salt; refrigerate until well chilled.
2. Combine remaining salt, 1 cup sour cream, lemon juice, onion, dill pickle, sugar, pepper and radishes. Toss cucumbers with this mixture. Refrigerate overnight.

**AT PARTY TIME:**

1. Arrange cold cucumbers on bed of lettuce. Garnish with 1 cup sour cream and sprinkle with parsley.

## *Potatissallad Med Ansjovis*
## *(Potato Salad with Anchovies)*

5 pounds new potatoes
1 bunch scallions, chopped
1 5-ounce can pimientos, drained and cut into strips
3 2-ounce cans anchovy fillets, drained and diced

¼ cup white vinegar
1 tablespoon lemon juice
¼ cup olive oil
Salt and freshly ground pepper to taste

**DAY BEFORE PARTY:**

1. Cover potatoes with boiling, salted water; bring to boil again and simmer for about 20 minutes, until just tender. Drain, peel, and cut in ¼" slices.
2. While potatoes are still warm, place in large bowl. Add scallions, pimientos, and anchovies.
3. Combine remaining ingredients and pour over potatoes. Toss gently to mix. Refrigerate overnight. Serve cold.

## *Hans-Notkott Platta*
## *(Ham and Roast Beef Plate)*

1 pound Virginia ham, sliced
1 pound lean roast beef, sliced

Cherry tomatoes
Parsley
2 hard-boiled eggs, sliced

**TWO HOURS BEFORE SERVING:**

1. Arrange ham and roast beef in triangles or rolls. Alternate on serving platter; garnish with tomatoes, parsley, and egg slices.

Cover with plastic wrap and reserve at room temperature until serving time.

# *Lök Paj*
## *(Onion Pie)*

2 cups flour
1 teaspoon salt
6 tablespoons butter
⅓ cup shortening
3 tablespoons milk
10 bacon slices
2½ cups thinly sliced onions

4 eggs
1⅓ cup sour cream
1 teaspoon salt
½ teaspoon white pepper
2 teaspoons fresh dill
1 teaspoon caraway seeds
1 teaspoon caraway seeds

**EARLY ON DAY OF PARTY:**
1. Preheat oven to 425°.
2. Sift flour and salt into bowl. With pastry blender or two knives, cut in butter and half of shortening until mixture is fine; cut in remaining shortening until particles are size of peas.
3. Sprinkle milk, a little at a time, over mixture, stirring with fork until dough clings together and cleans bowl. Shape dough into smooth ball.
4. On lightly floured board, roll dough into 14″ circle; fit into 11″ pie pan. Decorate edge; prick shell all over. Bake 10–12 minutes until golden brown. Let shell cool at room temperature.
5. Meanwhile, sauté bacon until crisp; crumble. In 4 tablespoons of bacon fat, sauté onions until tender.
6. In a bowl beat eggs and stir in sour cream, salt, pepper, dill, onions and bacon. Cover bowl with plastic wrap and refrigerate.

**AT PARTY TIME:**
1. Preheat oven to 300°. Pour egg-onion mixture into baked

pie shell. Sprinkle with caraway seeds. Bake 30 minutes. Let stand a few minutes before cutting into small wedges.

## *Kaaldolmer*
### *(Cabbage Leaves Stuffed with Meat)*

1 large cabbage
3 tablespoons rice
2 cups milk
¾ pound ground pork
¾ pound ground veal
1 teaspoon salt
7 egg whites
½ teaspoon ground white
   pepper

1 large onion, minced
2 cups beef consommé
½ cup molasses
1 tablespoon corn-
   starch
3 tablespoons water

**DAY BEFORE PARTY:**
1. Cut core from cabbage and cook in boiling, salted water for 15 minutes. Drain, cool slightly, and remove 30 large leaves.
2. Simmer rice in milk for 40 minutes. Cool.
3. Mix pork and veal with salt. With an electric beater, gradually blend in egg whites, one at a time. Then slowly beat in rice mixture to make a smooth filling. Stir in white pepper and minced onion.
4. Preheat oven to 375°.
5. Cut heavy part of stalk from cabbage leaves. Working with 1 leaf at a time, overlap slightly to close up opening where cut. Put tablespoon of meat filling on each leaf. Roll leaf over once, turn sides over filling and then roll to end of leaf, completely enclosing filling.
6. Arrange rolls in buttered baking dish. Add consommé and brush each roll with a little molasses. Bake for 30 minutes. Turn each roll carefully and bake 30 minutes more. Remove rolls with slotted spoon and arrange in serving dish.

7. Mix cornstarch and water and stir into liquid remaining in baking pan. Cook over direct heat, stirring for 2 minutes. Pour the sauce over Kaaldolmer. Let cool to room temperature. Cover and refrigerate.

**AT PARTY TIME:**
1. Remove Kaaldolmer from refrigerator 1 hour before serving.
2. Re-heat in 350° oven for 10–15 minutes or until warm through.

## *Små Köttbullar*
## *(Swedish Meatballs)*

3 or 4 slices white bread
1 cup milk
1 pound ground beef
½ pound ground veal
½ pound ground pork
2 eggs, slightly beaten
6 tablespoons chopped onion
1 tablespoon salt
½ teaspoon white pepper
½ teaspoon allspice

3 tablespoons butter
2 tablespoons oil
4 tablespoons flour
2 beef bouillon cubes
Boiling water
1 cup light cream
1 cup milk
2 tablespoons fresh chopped dill or 4 teaspoons dried dill

**DAY BEFORE PARTY:**
1. In blender, grate bread to make 1 cup fresh crumbs. Soak crumbs in milk about 5 minutes.
2. In large bowl, combine meats, eggs, onion, salt, pepper, allspice, and bread mixture. Toss gently with fork, just to combine. Gently shape mixture into 60 or 70 meatballs.
3. In skillet, heat butter and oil and sauté meatballs 10 or 15 at a time, until cooked through and browned. (About 10 minutes.) Remove meatballs as they are cooked and place in a large bowl.

When all meatballs are browned, remove skillet from heat.
4. Add flour to drippings in skillet, stirring until smooth. Add bouillon cubes; stir in 1½ cups boiling water.
5. Bring to boiling over medium heat, stirring until bouillon is dissolved and mixture is smooth. Add cream and milk. Simmer gently, stirring, for 3 minutes.
6. Add meatballs to sauce; toss gently to coat well. Simmer, covered, 5 minutes. Cool to room temperature. Cover and refrigerate.

**AT PARTY TIME:**
1. Remove meatballs from refrigerator 1 hour before serving.
2. Reheat gently until heated through and sauce is hot. Sprinkle with dill.

# *Kalvrulader*
## *(Stuffed Veal Rolls)*

4 pounds veal cutlets, cut
   in ¼" thick slices
3 teaspoons salt
1 teaspoon white pepper
2 sticks butter
2 cups chopped parsley
4 medium carrots, cut in
   1" chunks

4 medium onions, quartered
2 cans condensed beef
   bouillon, undiluted
2 tablespoons flour
1½ cups light cream
4 teaspoons granulated
   sugar

**DAY BEFORE PARTY:**
1. Cut veal into small serving pieces (about 3" × 4"). Sprinkle both sides with salt and pepper.
2. Melt ½ cup butter (1 stick); add parsley, spread a little of mixture on each piece of veal; roll up, tie with string.

3. In ½ cup hot butter in electric frying pan, sauté carrots, onions, and veal until meat is well browned.
4. Add water to bouillon to make 4 cups liquid; add to meat and vegetables; simmer, covered, 1 hour or until meat is fork tender. Turn veal into casserole; cover and refrigerate overnight.
5. Meanwhile, mash vegetables with fork in liquid in frying pan; gradually stir flour into cream; then stir into pan. Add ¼ teaspoon pepper and sugar; cook, stirring, just until heated. Taste for seasoning. Strain. Cool to room temperature and refrigerate.

**AT PARTY TIME:**
1. Remove veal rolls from refrigerator 1 hour before serving.
2. Arrange veal rolls in serving dish or baking dish. Pour gravy over them and re-heat for 15 minutes in 350° oven before serving.

## *Hasselbackpotatis*
### *(Roasted Potatoes)*

20 small baking potatoes
(about 2″ in diameter)
2 tablespoons soft butter
1 cup melted butter (2 sticks)

2 teaspoons salt
4 tablespoons breadcrumbs
4 tablespoons grated
Parmesan cheese

**EARLY ON DAY OF PARTY:**
1. Preheat oven to 425°. Peel potatoes. Place a potato on a wooden spoon that holds it comfortably. Beginning about ½″ from end, slice down at ¼″ intervals. (The spoon will prevent slicing all the way through.) Drop each semi-sliced potato into cold water to prevent discoloration.
2. When all potatoes are semi-sliced, drain and pat dry with paper towels.
3. Using 2 tablespoons butter, generously grease a large baking

dish and arrange potatoes cut side up, close together. (Don't stack.) Baste with ½ cup of melted butter; sprinkle with salt, and place in oven.

4. After 40 minutes sprinkle bread crumbs over potatoes and baste with remaining melted butter; roast 15 minutes more or until potatoes are just tender. Remove from oven. Set aside at room temperature.

**AT PARTY TIME:**
1. Sprinkle grated cheese on potatoes and re-heat in 350° oven for 20–25 minutes or until warmed through.

## *Bruna Bönor*
### *(Swedish Brown Beans)*

| | |
|---|---|
| 4 cups imported Swedish dried brown beans | 1 cup white vinegar |
| 11 cups water | 1 cup dark corn syrup |
| 3 teaspoons salt | 3 tablespoons brown sugar |

**DAY BEFORE PARTY:**
1. Wash beans thoroughly in cold, running water. (They will expand as they soak.) Place beans in large pot with 11 cups water. Bring to boil. Turn off heat and let beans soak, uncovered, for several hours.
2. Bring soaked beans to boil in same water, slightly cover pot and simmer over low heat for 1 hour. Stir in salt, vinegar, corn syrup and brown sugar, and continue cooking slowly. In another hour beans should be tender and sauce thick and brown. (Check periodically during cooking to make sure you don't overcook.)
3. If liquid evaporates too soon, add a little more water. Turn into ovenproof casserole. Cover and set aside at room temperature or refrigerate overnight.

**AT PARTY TIME:**
1. If beans have been refrigerated, let them come to room temperature one hour before serving.
2. Reheat for 15 minutes or until bubbling in 350° oven. (If necessary, add a little more water to keep from drying out.)

## *Socker Strutar*
## *(Sugar Cones)*

*For 30 Cones:*

1 cup granulated sugar
4 eggs, slightly beaten
10 tablespoons flour
1 teaspoon almond extract

4 cups heavy cream, whipped, flavored with 2 teaspoons sugar, 2 teaspoons vanilla
1 jar of lingonberries

**THREE OR FOUR DAYS BEFORE PARTY:**
1. Preheat oven to 425°. Grease and flour a cookie sheet.
2. In medium bowl, add sugar all at once to eggs. Beat until just smooth. Stir in flour gradually, then add almond extract; stir until blended.
3. Onto cookie sheet, drop one heaping tablespoon of mixture; with spoon, quickly spread into circle 4″ to 4½″ in diameter. Pour 2 or 3 more "pancakes." Bake about 3–4 minutes or until edge of circle is golden. With spatula, immediately remove from cookie sheet; quickly roll into cone shape. (Cone should be tightly rolled at bottom with about 2″ spread at the top.) Stand each cone up in a small glass until cool and firm. Lightly re-grease and flour sheet. Repeat procedure with remaining batter.
4. Store cones in tightly covered container.

**AT PARTY TIME:**
1. About 1 hour before guests arrive, place about 1 tablespoon flavored whipped cream in each cone; top with a teaspoon of

lingonberries. Serve standing up in small glasses. (Note: if you don't have room in your refrigerator for that many glasses, poke holes in an inverted box and prop the cones in the box.)

## *Expenses for a Walpurgis Night Smörgåsbord for 24–30*

| | |
|---|---|
| $ 40.00 | Aquavit (5 quarts) |
| 6.00 | Beer |
| 5.80 | Glasmästarsill (Glassblower's herring) |
| 6.35 | Sillisalaati (herring with sour cream) |
| 3.55 | Varm Krabbsmörgås (crabmeat canapés) |
| 9.45 | Gravad Lax (marinated salmon) |
| 1.05 | Pressgurka (cucumbers) |
| .60 | Lag Beta (pickled beets) |
| 5.00 | Lever Svenskt (Swedish liver pâté) |
| 1.35 | Gurka Surgrädde (cucumbers in sour cream) |
| 5.00 | Has-Notkott Platta (ham and roast beef plate) |
| 3.15 | Potatissallad med Ansjovis (potato salad with anchovies) |
| 2.10 | Lök Paj (onion pie) |
| 4.50 | Kaaldomer (stuffed cabbage) |
| 3.65 | Små Köttbullar (Swedish meatballs) |
| 16.15 | Kalvrulader (veal rolls) |
| .85 | Hasselbackpotatis (roasted potatoes) |
| 1.00 | Bruna Bönor (brown beans) |
| 2.55 | Socker Strutar (sugar cones) |
| 1.25 | Coffee |
| $133.80 | |

Entertain 30 guests at a splendid Smörgåsbord for $4.00 per person.

# An English Pub Party for 12

The English have graciously shared dozens of their customs and traditions with Americans—not the least of which is a common language. One institution, however, remains uniquely British, the typical English pub.

Of course there are American imitations with ceiling beams and pewter mugs for atmosphere and loaded with quasi-traditional English fare. But, basically, these are *restaurants*, not the ubiquitous English establishments where working men (and women) go to have a "nip and a nep" (beer and parsnips and turnips, but actually, a light lunch or supper).

English pubs are *not* sophisticated... they do not feature white-clothed tables and black-coated waiters serving $10.00 dinners. They are informal, warm, neighborhood bars where regulars drop in for a pint and some chow, good conversation and a rousing game of darts.

I think it's the camaraderie and congeniality of English pubs that makes them special. Although you personally lack the oak beams and aged pewter, it is possible (and a good deal of fun) to recapture that unique pub spirit... for one night anyway.

When you're telephoning invitations, stress the idea that this will be an informal evening, capped off with a marathon dart competition, and highlighted by pub specialties. Remember that English fare, of any class, is essentially hearty, so plan your pub party for any time from Fall through Spring, but eliminate the warmest months.

In terms of decor, you can't really recreate a pub, you can only approximate the setting. A family room or den is the ideal locale; the atmosphere should definitely not be formal. If you don't have a bar, set up a card table for the beverages, and a separate buffet arrangement for the food. Several little tables around the room, covered with checked cloths and flanked with straight chairs are appropriate for eating and drinking.

Most pubs have one chauvinist characteristic in common that you might adopt: a portrait of Queen Elizabeth. A local BOAC office or nearby British consulate can probably provide a hangable poster.

Plan for some music in tune with the atmosphere. Tom Jones (who actually started out as a pub singer) is fine, and so are any of the cockney singers belting English sing-along favorites (check your library for tapes or records). Some old rock tunes like *Winchester Cathedral* and Petula Clark's *Downtown* are also suitable, but the Beatles and the Rolling Stones, however English, don't really call forth the pub scene.

A very important aspect of the party is the dart board ... actually two dart boards, one for the ladies and one for the men. It's fun to have two games going, and then let the two winners of each game play each other. You might award small, but typically British prizes to the winners: perhaps tins of English biscuits, preserves, or tea to the top two men and women of the "playoff" game, and for the grand winner, a pewter or china mug.

If you're horrified at the idea of guests throwing darts at your papered, painted or panelled walls, it's easy enough to sidestep this problem with one or two sheets of masonite, very inexpensive and widely available at lumber yards or crafts shops. Secure the masonite to the wall with a couple of brads; then tack the dart boards to the masonite and your walls will remain unscathed.

Schedule the dart games before dinner while everyone is enjoying a brew and snacks (no pub would ever call them *hors d'oeuvres)* or wait until later when your guests are ready for some post-prandial exercise and competition.

The menu represents pub fare as closely as it's practical to do so, but there are some modifications necessary for the sake of American tastes. For example, about 80% of pub food is involved with pastry, either over, under, or all around the particular food. (Incidentally, in England a "pie" has pastry on top, a "tart" wears it on the bottom, and a "pasty" is completely enclosed. A "pudding" is usually a pastry dish that is boiled or steamed instead of baked.) This plethora of pastry can get a little heavy and a little boring, so we eliminated sausage rolls, pork pies, toad-in-the-hole (sausage pie), and kidney pasties as possible starters, leaving the field open to Cornish pasties as an appetizer, and selecting two among dozens of traditional pies as main courses.

Instead of any of the wonderful pastries and turnovers usually featured as pub desserts (apple and plum, mince, molasses, berries) we've substituted two special English favorites: Maids of Honour (which are cheese tarts, but more cheese than tart) and Tipsy Cake (otherwise known as Trifle) a delightful concoction of lady-fingers, custard and preserves cum brandy.

Then too, American ladies may not be as fond of a pint as their British counterparts, so we offer gin with bitter orange (much more popular in England than the bitter lemon variety) in addition to three kinds of beer.

We're also eschewing one other pub tradition, still practiced in smaller towns and villages: often, the ladies are only permitted to drink in the "saloon" portion of a pub where the atmosphere is supposedly more genteel than in the "public" section.

So, with a cheer of "Long Live The Queen," here's the menu for an

# English Pub Party for 12

Ale, Lager and Stout

Gin with Bitters

Gin and Bitter Orange

### Appetizers

Stilton Cheese

Double Gloucester Cheese

English Biscuits (Crackers)

Potted Salmon        Pickled Eggs        Individual Cornish Pasties

### Main Course

Beefsteak, Kidney & Mushroom Pie        Cornish Chicken Pie

Bubble & Squeak        Stuffed Onions
(Cabbage and Potatoes)

Tomato Plus Saladings

### Desserts

Maids of Honour Tarts        Tipsy Cake (Trifle)

English Tea

Mead        Port

## Beverages

A pub without beer would be rather like a hospital without medicine. For your pub party, offer a choice of beers. Most American palates are accustomed to what the British know as lager beers, the lightest type. The English add a squirt of lime juice to lager to make it a little more interesting.

Slightly racier than lager beer is ale; then comes porter, still a little darker and sweeter, and finally stout, the richest and sweetest of all. English like "half and half" which is stout mixed with ale. Your beer selection should include domestic lager, either imported or domestic ale, and imported stout (Guinness is widely available; your liquor dealer can also order other brands).

Contrary to popular opinion, beer shouldn't be served too cold—the best temperature is about 50°. Ale should be chilled even less; stout and porter aren't chilled at all. To serve any of these, chill the mugs first, then pour the beer.

Schweppe's Bitter Orange is as common as Coke in England . . . but rather difficult to come by here. For the Gin and Orange drinkers substitute Cott's Orange Dry, or if you can't get that, provide plain old orange soda (a good brand that's not too sweet).

A word about Mead which we've listed as an after dinner drink. Mead is a sweet-ish honey wine reputed in the old days to be an elixir to prolong life. In fact, the word "honeymoon" comes from the practice of Goths drinking mead for one full month after a wedding. Mead is available in the U.S. (Bandor, ironically made in Denmark, is one good brand), but for fun, try making your own by following this simple recipe:

## Honey Mead

| | |
|---|---|
| 1 pound granulated sugar | 4 cloves |
| 1 gallon water | 1 teaspoon rosemary |

| | |
|---|---|
| 4 cups clear honey | 1 3-inch stick of ginger |
| 2 lemons | 1 ounce yeast spread on a slice of white toast |

**ONE MONTH BEFORE SERVING:**

1. Boil together sugar, water, honey and skim off any scum that rises.
2. Let stand in a glass bowl and add the juice of 2 lemons, and the rind of one lemon. Add cloves, rosemary, and crushed ginger.
3. When mixture has cooled to room temperature, add the yeast on toast. Cover bowl with a piece of muslin or a thin towel.
4. Let the mead ferment for about a week (remove lemon peel after 4 days). When it stops "hissing" (after about a week), strain and bottle. Cork tightly and leave for about two more weeks before drinking . . . the longer, the better.

## *Cheese Tray*

| | |
|---|---|
| 1 Pound Stilton Cheese | English Biscuits (Carr's |
| 1 Pound Double Gloucester | Wheatmeal or Water Biscuits, or Fortt's Bath Olivers) |

**ONE HOUR BEFORE SERVING:**

1. Cut part of each cheese (about half) into bite-sized wedges; arrange on tray with biscuits. Let stand with remaining cheese at room temperature until serving.
(In England, some people spoon Stilton with a silver spoon, but experts say it should be enjoyed in wedges. Stilton is the blue-veined cousin of Roquefort, Gorgonzola, and Bleu cheese; Double Gloucester is related to Cheddar cheese, but has a stronger, yet smoother taste.)

# Potted Salmon or Tuna Fish

2 cans salmon or tuna fish,
 drained
4 tablespoons anchovy paste
½ pound butter, melted

Salt and cayenne pepper to
 taste
Pinch of mace
1 sweet pickle, thinly sliced

**DAY BEFORE PARTY:**
1. Add fish, anchovy paste, and butter to blender container. Whirl briefly until mixture is creamy.
2. Add seasoning but take it easy on the salt! Turn into a serving bowl, cover with plastic wrap and refrigerate.

**AT PARTY TIME:**
1. Remove potted fish from refrigerator one hour before serving. Arrange pickle slices on top of fish. Serve with biscuits.

# Pickled Eggs

2 cups white vinegar
2 teaspoons ground ginger
2 teaspoons pickling spice
12 whole black peppers

12 hard-boiled eggs, shelled
1 large onion, sliced
3 cloves garlic
1 teaspoon dried dill

**FOUR OR FIVE DAYS BEFORE PARTY:**
1. In small saucepan, bring vinegar, ginger, pickling spice and black peppers to a boil. Then lower heat and simmer 5 minutes.
2. Pour hot mixture over eggs in a 1-quart jar. (If this doesn't cover eggs, add a little more water).
3. Add onion, garlic and dill weed. Refrigerate, covered, four or five days.

**AT PARTY TIME:**
1. Cut eggs in wedges; sprinkle with salt, pepper, and paprika.

# *Individual Cornish Pasties*

Traditionally, Cornish pasties were marked at one end with the initials of the family members or guests who would be eating them. A person would begin eating the unmarked end so that if any was left over, each could find his own pastie. Our version, made in miniature form, is a delightful pub-style hors d'oeuvre . . . and we doubt that any will be left over, but we've included the initials for fun and tradition.

1 double recipe for pie crust or 2 packages pie crust mix
1 large onion, chopped
1 tablespoon vegetable oil
1 1-pound can corned beef hash

1 egg, beaten
1 tablespoon Worcestershire sauce
1 egg, beaten, or 3 tablespoons cream for glazing pastry

**DAY BEFORE PARTY OR EARLY ON PARTY DAY:**
1. Prepare filling: Sauté onion in oil until tender. Remove from heat. Drain off excess oil. Mix hash with onion, egg, and Worcestershire sauce. Set aside.
2. Make pastry. Divide dough in half for easier handling. Refrigerate un-used half. Roll dough out on floured board and cut into 12 3″ or 4″ rounds.
3. Place about 1 tablespoon of filling in the center of each round. Wet edges of pastry with brush and flip over into half circle shape. Crimp edges with fork, or trim with a pastry cutter. On 1 corner, using a shrimp fork or hat pin, prick appropriate initials on each pastry. Then brush each with egg or cream and set on cookie sheet. Continue with remaining pastry. You should have 2 pasties for each guest.
4. Preheat oven to 375°; bake pasties about 30 minutes or until golden brown.

5. If made the same day as party, store at room temperature. If made the day before, cool and refrigerate. (The pasties may also be made 1 or 2 weeks ahead and frozen. Defrost for 1 hour before reheating.)

**AT PARTY TIME:**
1. Reheat pasties for 10 or 15 minutes in preheated 300° oven.
2. Serve hot, but don't worry if they cool off a bit. In England, pasties are usually eaten cold; in fact, a traditional lunch-box meal is a man-sized meat tart with any of several savory fillings.

## Beefsteak, Kidney and Mushroom Pie

You won't find two cooks who agree exactly on the preparation, nor two restaurants that serve exactly the same version. This is our favorite formula. (If you're queasy about kidneys, leave them out!)

1 teaspoon salt
½ teaspoon freshly ground
  pepper
1 cup flour
2 pounds round steak, cut
  into ¾″ cubes
½ pound veal, beef, or lamb
  kidneys, in thin slices
2 tablespoons corn oil
¼ cup chopped onion

½ pound mushrooms,
  chopped
2 cups beef consommé
2 tablespoons chopped
  parsley
1 tablespoon Worcestershire
  sauce
1 package frozen patty shells
1 slightly beaten egg for glaze

**EARLY ON PARTY DAY:**
1. Add salt and pepper to flour in a paper or plastic bag. Coat steak cubes and kidneys with flour.

2.  Heat oil in an electric skillet or large frying pan; brown about half the meat on all sides; remove from skillet. Then brown remaining meat and set aside.

3.  In same skillet, sauté onions until almost tender, add mushrooms and sauté for 2 minutes more.

4.  Return steak and kidneys to frying pan; add consommé, parsley, and Worcestershire sauce. Simmer for about 1½ hours, covered, until meat is tender. Adjust seasoning.

5.  Meanwhile, defrost patty shells. On floured board or plastic wrap, roll shells together to fit the top of a deep, large casserole or soufflé dish (about 10″ across). Cut a 1″ hole in the center. With pastry scraps make 5 or 6 decorative leaves to embellish top of crust. Refrigerate crust and leaves until ready to use.

6.  When meat is tender turn into casserole or soufflé dish. Top with prepared crust. Place a small funnel in center hole so steam will escape. Place pastry leaves attractively on crust. Brush with beaten egg.

7.  Bake in preheated 425° oven for 45 minutes or until top is golden brown. Remove from oven and let stand at room temperature.

**AT PARTY TIME:**
1.  Reheat 10 or 15 minutes in 300° oven or until heated through.

## *Cornish Chicken Pie*

1 4–5 pound soup chicken,
  cut up
2 carrots, peeled and cut
  in chunks
2 stalks celery, cut in chunks
2 teaspoons salt
1 teaspoon pepper
8 slices Virginia ham, cut
  ¼″ thick

1 teaspoon sugar
½ teaspoon dried dill
1½ cups chicken stock
3 tablespoons butter
3 tablespoons flour
pastry for a 10-inch crust
  (half a regular pie crust
  recipe, or ½ box of pie
  crust mix.)

½ cup fresh chopped parsley
1 medium-sized onion, minced
1 teaspoon salt
½ teaspoon white pepper

1 egg, beaten, for glaze or use a few tablespoons of cream
1 cup half and half (or use half heavy cream, half milk, or use light cream)

**DAY BEFORE PARTY:**
1. Stew chicken, with enough water to cover plus carrots, celery, salt and pepper for 1½ hours. Let cool. Remove chicken from broth. Heat broth over high heat until reduced to about 3 cups. Refrigerate or place in freezer so that fat will rise to top. (Discard vegetables.)
2. Bone chicken and cut in bite sized pieces.
3. In a 2″ deep casserole or baking dish, place one layer of ham (use two slices). Mix parsley, onion, salt, pepper, sugar, and dill together. Sprinkle about one-third of this mixture on ham slices. Then add a layer of chicken, again using about one-third. Repeat ham slices, onion mixture, and chicken layers twice more. End with a layer of ham. Set aside.
4. Skim fat from chicken stock. Reheat 1½ cups; reserve remaining stock for other uses.
5. In a separate saucepan melt the butter and blend in the flour. Add the hot stock all at once, stirring with a wire whisk. Cook until thick and smooth. Pour into chicken-ham mixture.
6. Roll out pastry on floured board; cut a fairly large hole about 1 or 1½″ in center. Prick pastry with a fork and add a funnel to the hole to let steam escape.
7. Preheat oven to 425°. Brush pastry with a beaten egg or use a few tablespoons of half-and-half to glaze. Bake pie in oven for 15 minutes at 425°; then lower heat to 300° and cook for 45 minutes longer or until crust is golden. Remove from oven and set aside at room temperature. When cool, cover and refrigerate until party time.

**AT PARTY TIME:**
1. Preheat oven to 300°. Remove pie from refrigerator 1 hour before serving. In small saucepan, gently heat the half-and-half.
2. Reheat pie for 20 minutes or until heated through. Just before serving pour hot cream into the small hole on top. Serve immediately.

# Bubble and Squeak
## (Potatoes and Cabbage)

2 tablespoons bacon grease
3 tablespoons butter
8 large cooked potatoes, riced
1 medium cabbage, shredded as for cole slaw
Salt and pepper to taste

**EARLY ON DAY OF PARTY:**
1. Heat bacon fat and butter in skillet. Meanwhile, combine potatoes and cabbage with a little salt and pepper. When fat is hot, add potato-cabbage mixture and fry. The secret of making Bubble and Squeak is to keep turning mixture so it cooks through and through without browning or forming a crust. Literally, it's supposed to bubble and squeak while you cook. When potatoes are tender, remove from heat. Adjust seasoning. Turn into serving casserole. Set aside at room temperature.

**AT PARTY TIME:**
1. Reheat Bubble and Squeak in 300° oven for 10 or 15 minutes or until heated through.

# Stuffed Onions

12 medium onions, about 2″ in diameter
¼ cup corn oil or 2 table-
2 tablespoons chopped parsley
¾ cup breadcrumbs

spoons butter and 2 tablespoons oil
2 tablespoons finely chopped
celery
⅓ cup chopped mushrooms

1 egg, beaten
salt and freshly ground black
pepper to taste
⅔ teaspoon beef extract
(Bovril)
4 teaspoons flour

## DAY BEFORE PARTY:

1. Peel onions. Cut a ½″ diameter slice off bottom of each onion so onion will stand; cut a slice 1¼″ in diameter from top of each onion. Discard. Simmer onions in 1 quart of boiling water for 15 minutes. Remove from water and drain, reserving stock. With a shrimp fork, gently ease out centers of onions; discard centers of 5 onions; mince remainder.
2. Heat oil or oil/butter in frying pan, add minced onions and celery. When onions are golden, add mushrooms and sauté another minute or two until mushrooms are lightly browned.
3. Remove from heat. Add parsley, breadcrumbs, egg and salt and pepper. Mix well. Adjust seasoning.
4. Stuff onion shells; place in a lightly greased baking dish.
5. Stir beef extract into onion stock, thicken with 4 teaspoons flour, bring to a boil and boil for 3 minutes, stirring occasionally. Pour stock over onions and bake one hour at 300° or until tender. Baste several times during cooking. Cool at room temperature; refrigerate.

## AT PARTY TIME:

1. One hour before serving, remove from refrigerator.
2. In a 300° oven, reheat onions for 10 or 15 minutes or until stock is bubbling and onions are heated through.

# Tomato Plus Saladings

1 pint cherry tomatoes
1 bunch radishes
1 bunch scallions
3 or 4 carrots cut into sticks
4 or 5 celery stalks, cut
  into sticks

Lettuce or watercress
¼ cup vegetable oil
2 tablespoons lemon juice
2 tablespoons white vinegar
Salt and pepper

**EARLY ON DAY OF PARTY:**
1. Prepare vegetables; arrange on a bed of lettuce or watercress and refrigerate.
2. Mix oil, lemon juice, vinegar and salt and pepper together in a glass jar. Cover and shake well.

**AT PARTY TIME:**
1. Sprinkle vegetables with additional salt and pepper; pour dressing over and serve.

# Maids of Honour Tarts

Maids of Honour were first introduced as a dessert by George II of England who named the pastry after the queen's ladies-in-waiting. These succulent little tarts are actually an English version of cheesecake, and bear great resemblance to the Italian Ricotta pie.

1½ times the quantity of your
  favorite pastry recipe; or
  use 1½ boxes of pie crust
  mix
3 eggs
1½ cups creamed cottage
  cheese

½ cup sugar
½ cup heavy cream
1 tablespoon lemon juice
1 tablespoon flour
¼ teaspoon salt
2 tablespoons ground
  almonds

**DAY BEFORE PARTY:**
1. Prepare pastry. Divide dough in half. Refrigerate half. On floured board, roll out dough to a square about 15″ × 15″. Using a 2¼″ cookie cutter or small glass, cut about 40 rounds. Re-roll pastry scraps to make additional rounds. Repeat with remaining dough. You should have 80 or more rounds.
2. Preheat oven to 425°.
3. Grease 2 muffin tins. Place 1 round in bottom of each muffin "cup," then press 4 more rounds in petal pattern into each muffin cup. You should have at least 16 pastry cups. Prick all over with fork and bake 10 minutes until just beginning to brown. Remove from oven.
4. Place remaining ingredients (except ground almonds) in blender container and blend for 1 minute until very smooth.
5. Turn egg-cheese mixture into prepared tarts and bake in 350° oven for 30–40 minutes or until puffy. Cool to room temperature and sprinkle with ground almonds. Refrigerate overnight.

**AT PARTY TIME:**
1. Remove from refrigerator 1 hour before serving. If desired, reheat slightly for 10 minutes in 200° oven, but Maid of Honour tarts can also be served cool—not *cold*, however!

## Tipsy Cake: Trifle

2 packages lady fingers
½ cup apricot preserves
½ cup strawberry preserves
½ cup brandy
¼ cup sherry
2 tablespoons sugar

4 cups milk
8 egg yolks, beaten
1 teaspoon almond extract
½ pint heavy cream, whipped
   with 1 teaspoon sugar
Grated almonds for garnish

**EARLY ON DAY OF PARTY:**
1. Split lady fingers; spread half with apricot jam and the remainder with strawberry preserves. Sprinkle lady fingers with brandy and sherry. Let soak for about ½ an hour.
2. Meanwhile, make custard: In a double boiler, add sugar to milk; bring to a scald and beat in egg yolks. Cook mixture over hot water, stirring constantly until custard begins to thicken. When it coats the back of a spoon, remove from heat and add almond extract. Set aside.
3. In individual parfait glasses, champagne glasses, or sherbet dishes (lacking any of these, arrange the trifle in one big casserole), place a few apricot-lady fingers, and a bit of custard; then a few strawberry-lady fingers and custard, etc., until lady fingers and custard are evenly distributed. Refrigerate.

**AT PARTY TIME:**
1. Top each serving with whipped cream, sprinkle with grated almonds; serve cold.

## Expenses for English Pub Party for 12:

| | |
|---|---|
| $ 9.00 | Ale, Lager, Stout |
| 3.00 | Gin with bitters |
| 5.50 | Gin with Bitter Orange |
| 2.50 | Stilton Cheese |
| 3.00 | Double Gloucester Cheese |
| 2.00 | English Biscuits |
| 1.70 | Potted Salmon |
| 1.50 | Pickled Eggs |
| 1.55 | Individual Cornish Pasties |
| 5.85 | Beefsteak, Kidney & Mushroom Pie |
| 6.20 | Cornish Chicken Pie |
| .85 | Bubble and Squeak (cabbage and potatoes) |

|         |                        |
|---------|------------------------|
| 1.10    | Stuffed Onions         |
| 2.00    | Tomato plus Saladings  |
| 1.10    | Maids of Honour Tarts  |
| 5.15    | Tipsy Cake (Trifle)    |
| .75     | English Tea            |
| 3.00    | Mead                   |
| 6.50    | Port                   |
| $62.25  |                        |

For $5.00 a person you can recapture the spirit of an English Pub for 12 guests.

# Say "Kung-Hsi" with a
# Chinese New Year's Party for 18–24

Among all the world's cuisines, Chinese food shares the pinnacle with one or two others. (Some say France and China occupy the top spot; others say both France and Italy, along with China hold equal rating; but China's position is never challenged by international epicures.)

There are a good many reasons for this claim to fame, but one the most important is that to the Chinese, cooking is an art, not a craft. Confucius himself laid down some of the rules about food—it had to be fresh and tastefully prepared, as well as attractively served.•Everything must be balanced in texture, flavor, aroma, and color.

Further, Confucius felt eating was an integral aspect of the Chinese social order. When men feasted together, sharing good food, it was symbolic of the harmony of life preached by the philosopher. Food and friendship became inseparable.

Accordingly, good cooking is so significant in China that there are five different "schools" of cuisine, each with characteristic specialties: Manchurian, Pekinese, Cantonese, Fukienese, and Szechwan. (Peking used to be the most famous province for food in China; all chefs went there to learn the trade.) In the United States Cantonese food for many years was the most popular, but in recent years, Szechwan cooking with its hot, peppery dishes, is the rage. I think at least one new Szechwan restaurant opens in New York City every month.

Aside from the regional variations, there are three distinct types of Chinese fare. 1. Unadorned food, accompanied only by a little spice or a light sauce (in the way we would serve steak or lobster); 2. Food that's been transformed with tricky sauces and combinations of spices somewhat like French cooking; 3. A melange of main ingredients and vegetables, spices and sauces that through a happy marriage becomes an unusual total creation, not just a disguised collection of tid-bits.

The Chinese are so hipped on food that it has been observed they invented the mid-morning snack as a way of relieving the monotony of not eating!

A good example of the relation of food to Chinese culture is the celebration of New Year, the favorite Chinese holiday. Traditional dishes are as vital as the dragon dances, fireworks and other joyous customs of the season. While it would be difficult to stage an authentic Chinese New Year's feast at home (think of all those firecrackers!), it is possible to capture the spirit of the event.

First off, the Chinese New Year occurs any time between January 21 and February 19th, depending on the first day of the new moon. (Although the Chinese follow the Western calendar, for the holidays and other traditional ceremonies they use the ancient lunar calendar.) Since the gala celebrations go on for much longer than one day—often as long as three weeks—you can schedule your own party anytime during that interim. Festivities begin a week before the new moon when the family says goodbye to the God of the Hearth (The Kitchen God) who departs to make his annual report to the Jade Emperor, the Ruler of Heaven, on the conduct of the household.

Before the Kitchen God leaves on his celestial visit, his picture is coated with syrup so he'll have nothing but sweet things to say to the Emperor. As part of the ceremony, the picture is placed in a mini sedan chair and then set afire, while tea and wine are poured on the flames so the God won't be thirsty. A week later, on New Year's Eve, a new picture of the Kitchen God is hung in the kitchen to symbolize his return.

For the last two or three days of the old year, a cellar to attic cleaning is the rule, a ritual that ranks with the American version of spring cleaning for effort and thoroughness. While the women scrub, the husbands are busy repaying any debts, another tradition of the season.

Many hours are spent preparing food, both for ancestors and for living guests. One customary snack for New Year's visitors is "Chungun," known as egg rolls to Western fans of Chinese food, but called Spring rolls by the Chinese, because they are made to welcome in the spring which begins the day after New Year's.

During the holiday, businesses close for at least three days; in more leisurely times, some lucky people would take a month's vacation to celebrate the New Year. Everyone wears his best clothes, and tries to avoid talking of unpleasant things—a happy philosophy for any culture to observe.

On New Year's Day, there's always a parade with a large papier maché dragon. New York's Chinatown claims the grandest celebrations outside of China, but this claim is disputed by San Francisco, where they have been celebrating Chinese New Year's since 1851, complete with a block-long dragon dance.

After the parades and street-side activities, feasting is in order. At each home one virtually sees red, since this color signifies good luck and joy. Crimson lanterns and red paper scrolls abound; children and grown-up guests alike receive little red envelopes called "hung bows" filled with two coins as dictated by the Chinese tradition that everything good comes in twos.

Aside from the red decorations, every home has incense burning in tribute to ancestors and platters of grapefruit, oranges, and tangerines are arranged in pyramids as a sign of abundance. Bouquets of orange blossoms also signify profit and plenty for the coming year.

An important part of the celebrations and decorations involves whichever animal symbolizes the New Year. Each year is represented by a different creature corresponding to each of the 12 zodiac signs. 1973, for example is The Year of The Ox or Cow (Taurus); 1974, The Tiger (Gemini); 1975, The Hare (Cancer); 1976, The Dragon (Leo); 1977, The Snake (Virgo); 1978, The Horse, (Libra); 1979, The Sheep (Scorpio); 1980, The Monkey (Sagittarius); 1981, The Cock (Capricorn); 1982, The Dog (Aquarius); 1983, The Boar (Pisces); 1984, The Rat (Aries), and 1985 would once again be The Year of The Ox.

The visiting and feasting for the New Year goes on until the full moon, 14 days later, when the celebration comes to an end with the "Feast of Lanterns" and everyone settles down to ordinary occupations for the rest of the year.

For your own Chinese New Year's Party, start with invitations that portray the animal of the year. Chinese markets or import shops carry little cards with the symbolic creatures. (While you're at it, you might want to try to find some large posters of the featured animal as keynotes for your decorations.) On your invitation, be sure to include either the phrase "kung-hsi," meaning "happy greetings" or "fa-ts'ai," "may you gather wealth."

You can follow the Chinese traditions closely in terms of decor with an abundance of red (tablecloth and napkins), the characteristic incense, pyramids of fresh fruit and hanging lanterns. For fun, give every guest his own "hung bow" envelope containing two coins. If you have a fireplace you could even burn the Kitchen God early in the evening and replace him with a new picture (that of your husband, perhaps) later on.

The menu is appropriately lavish and includes favorites from several schools of cooking. We've taken some liberties, however, in the preparation of the food, since so many Chinese dishes are prepared in the stir-fry method, immediately before serving, which doesn't work well for entertaining purposes.

Here's the bill of fare for a New Year's party that will gather many "kung-hsi" for you as a hostess:

# Chinese New Years Party for 18–24

Shao Hsing Wine                      Kirin Beer
*(served before and during dinner)*

## Dien-Hsing ("strike the heart")
### (Appetizers)

Yang Chow Haah Kow            Char Siu
*(fried shrimp balls)*     *(cold pork with mustard sauce)*

Shew Pye Gult            Yeung Doong Gwoo
*(barbecued spareribs)*     *(stuffed mushrooms)*

Chungun                Bo-Pe
*(spring rolls)*        *(stuffed dumplings)*

## Ching Chan
### (Main Course)

Haap To Ghuy           Tim Sun Gnow
*(chicken with walnuts)*     *(sweet and sour beef)*

For Toi Chow Fan          Jow Mein
*(precious fried rice)*      *(fried noodles)*

Baak Fan
*(Steamed Rice)*

### (Dessert)

Jih Maah Baang         Hung Yun Beang
*(sesame seed cookies)*    *(Chinese almond cakes)*

*(fortune cookies)*

Jasmine Tea

# Yang Chow Haah Kow
## *(Fried Shrimp Balls)*

4 pounds raw shrimp, shelled
  and deveined
¼ pound pork fat
6 water chestnuts
2 scallions or 1 small onion
5 egg whites, slightly beaten
¾ cup sifted flour

½ teaspoon salt
½ teaspoon white pepper
Dash of ginger powder
2 tablespoons ice water
1 tablespoon sherry
½ cup cornstarch

Peanut oil for deep frying

**DAY BEFORE PARTY:**
1. Chop together (very finely) the shrimp, fat, water chestnuts and onions.
2. Blend in egg whites, flour, salt, pepper, ginger, ice water, and sherry. Mix by hand until mixture begins to turn pink. Then slap "dough" on hard surface until pasty. Shape into walnut-sized balls. Roll in cornstarch.
3. Heat peanut oil to 360° and fry balls until puffed and golden. Drain on paper towels. Makes about 45 balls. Place in baking tin; cover with aluminum foil and refrigerate.

**AT PARTY TIME:**
1. Remove balls from refrigerator about 1 hour before serving.
2. With foil cover still on, heat in 250° oven for 10 to 15 minutes or until warmed through.

# Char Siu
## *(Cold Pork with Mustard Sauce)*

4 pound boneless pork roast
*Sauce:* mix together:
  2 cups soy sauce

Chinese style hot mustard

1 cup sherry
1 cup brown sugar
2 teaspoons salt
¼ teaspoon pepper
¼ teaspoon monosodium glutamate (msg)
2 medium onions, diced

**DAY BEFORE PARTY:**
1. Place pork roast in roasting pan. Cover with sauce and marinate 4 or 5 hours, turning several times.
2. Preheat oven to 400°. Place pork on rack in same pan with marinade and roast for 15 minutes.
3. Lower heat to 325°. Continue roasting for 2 more hours or until meat thermometer registers 185°. Baste frequently. (Add water, if necessary.)
4. Let cool to room temperature; then refrigerate overnight.

**AT PARTY TIME:**
1. 30 minutes before serving, remove roast from refrigerator and slice in ⅛" pieces. Then cut each slice to rectangles 2-2½" long by an inch wide (or whatever is economically sensible).
2. Arrange on a platter with mustard in the center for dipping.

## *Shew Pye Gult*
### *(Barbecued Spareribs)*

½ cup soy sauce
2 tablespoons sherry
2 tablespoons honey
6 tablespoons pineapple juice
2 teaspoons peanut oil

2 teaspoons salt
2 teaspoons sugar
2 teaspoons corn oil
2 teaspoons minced garlic
2 teaspoons minced fresh
     ginger

4 racks spareribs, cut into individual ribs

**DAY BEFORE PARTY:**
1. Combine all ingredients for the marinade. Then add the ribs and marinate overnight, turning several times.
**THREE HOURS BEFORE SERVING:**
1. Drain spareribs, reserving marinade. Place ribs on a rack in a shallow roasting pan. (You will probably have to use two pans; if so, keep interchanging position in oven to cook evenly.)
2. Roast in 350° preheated oven for 1 hour pouring off fat and basting frequently with the marinade. If ribs aren't getting crispy enough raise heat to 375° or 400° for the last 10 minutes. Let stand at room temperature until ready to serve.
3. Reheat briefly in 250° oven before serving.

## *Yeung Doong Gwoo*
### *(Stuffed Mushrooms)*

48 large dried mushroom caps
1 pound crabmeat, fresh or frozen
10 water chestnuts, minced
2 egg whites, lightly beaten

2 tablespoons cornstarch
2 tablespoons soy sauce
2 tablespoons sherry
¼ teaspoon msg
2 scallions, minced

**EARLY ON DAY OF PARTY:**
1. Clean mushrooms in cool water. Remove stems. Soak in water several hours. Squeeze dry before using.
2. Mix crabmeat, water chestnuts, and egg white. Sprinkle with cornstarch. Mix soy sauce, sherry, msg, and scallions. Add to crabmeat mixture.
3. Fill mushroom caps with crabmeat mixture.
4. Steam for 40 minutes. (Adapt a steamer by adding a cake cooling rack to an electric frying pan; fill pan with about ¾" of water and set control for simmer. If you don't have a suitable

rack, perforate an aluminum pie tin with a fork and use that as a base for the mushrooms. You will probably have to steam the mushrooms half at a time.) Set aside at room temperature.

**AT PARTY TIME:**
1. Reheat covered mushrooms in 250–300° oven for 5–10 minutes or until warmed through.

# *Chungun*
## *(Spring Rolls—Egg Rolls)*

### FIRST MAKE FILLINGS:

#### *Pork-Shrimp Filling*

3 tablespoons peanut oil
½ pound pork, cut in julienne strips
½ pound raw shrimp, shelled, deveined and diced
9 minced water chestnuts

½ cup finely chopped scallions
1 tablespoons soy sauce
1 teaspoon salt
1 teaspoon sherry

**DAY BEFORE PARTY:**
1. Heat oil in skillet. Sauté pork for 4 or 5 minutes, stirring often.
2. Combine shrimp with remaining ingredients; add to skillet; cook, stirring until shrimp turns pink (about 4 or 5 minutes). Set aside.

#### *Chicken Filling*

1 raw, skinned and boned chicken breast
1 teaspoon cornstarch

4 scallions, chopped
1 cup fresh or canned bean sprouts

½ teaspoon salt
½ teaspoon sugar
2 tablespoons soy sauce
2 tablespoons peanut oil

½ cup diced fresh or canned
   bamboo shoots
1 teaspoon sherry

**DAY BEFORE PARTY:**
1. Cut chicken in very narrow strips. Mix with cornstarch, salt, sugar, and 1 tablespoon soy sauce. Let stand 15 minutes.
2. Heat 1 tablespoon oil in skillet; sauté scallions, bean sprouts, and bamboo shoots for 3 minutes. Season with remaining soy sauce and remove from pan.
3. Heat remaining oil in skillet; sauté chicken 2 minutes.
4. Return vegetables, add sherry and cook 2 more minutes; chill for half an hour before filling "skins."

*PREPARE SKINS:* You can purchase "skins" in a Chinese market or in some specialty food stores. If you can't find them, use this dough:

2 eggs, lightly beaten
4 cups sifted flour

1 teaspoon salt
1 cup very cold water

**DAY BEFORE PARTY:**
1. Save about 1 tablespoon of the egg for sealing the rolls. Combine remaining egg with other ingredients to make dough. Work in well, cover and let stand for 15 minutes.
2. Knead dough until smooth and elastic. Divide in half. Divide each half into 18 pieces; roll each piece out into a 6-inch square and fill.

*TO ASSEMBLE ROLLS:*
Peanut oil for deep frying
36 "skins"

Pork Shrimp Filling
Chicken Filling
Reserved egg from home-
   made dough, or 1 egg,
   lightly beaten

1. Heat oil in electric skillet or deep fryer to temperature of 375°. While oil is heating, prepare rolls.
2. On each "skin" place 1 tablespoon filling in the center. Fold and roll; tuck in the sides; seal edges with reserved egg.
3. Fry 4 or 5 rolls at a time until golden brown (about 5 minutes). Drain well on paper towels.
4. When all rolls are cooked, turn into foil pan; cover with foil and refrigerate overnight.

**AT PARTY TIME:**
1. Remove from refrigerator 1 hour before serving.
2. Re-heat in 250–300° for 10 minutes or until warmed through.

# Bo-Pe
## (Stuffed Dumplings)

4 cups flour
2 tablespoon sugar
1 teaspoon salt
1 package yeast dissolved in
  1½ cups warm water
2 tablespoons melted
  shortening

**Meat Filling: mix together**
½ pound ground beef
¼ pound chopped
  mushrooms
2 large stalks celery, minced
2 scallions, minced
Salt and pepper to taste

**DAY BEFORE PARTY:**
1. Sift flour, sugar, and salt together in large bowl; make well in center. Add yeast, melted shortening and mix well together.
2. Knead lightly on floured board until dough is smooth and elastic. Then place in greased bowl; cover with a sheet of waxed paper and let rise at room temperature about 3 hours.
3. Oil hands and board with salad oil and divide dough into 24 small portions. Press out with hands and then roll with floured rolling pin until each piece is about 4" in diameter.

4. Drop a tablespoon of filling onto each piece of dough; then draw up edges around filling to make into a ball. Press edges together and turn so seams are underneath. Let rise double.
5. Bake, fry, or steam on rack (Bake at 400° for 20 minutes; fry in deep fat at 375° until golden; or steam over boiling water 30 minutes.) When cooked, cover and refrigerate overnight.

**AT PARTY TIME:**
1. Remove Bo-Pe from refrigerator 1 hour before serving.
2. Re-heat, covered, in a 250°–300° oven until heated through (about 10 or 15 minutes).

## Haap To Ghuy
### (Chicken with Walnuts)

2 cups shelled walnuts
3 pounds of boned chicken
   breasts
2 teaspoons salt
2 teaspoons sugar
½ cup sherry
2 tablespoons soy sauce
2 tablespoons honey
6 tablespoons cornstarch

2 eggs, beaten
½ cup peanut oil
4 teaspoons minced ginger
   root
3 minced garlic cloves
1 cup boiling water
1 teaspoon msg
2 cups sliced bamboo shoots

**DAY BEFORE PARTY:**
1. Blanch walnuts by pouring boiling water over them. Let stand 10 minutes. Drain; place in cold water. Slip off skins, if there are any. Drain on paper towels. Set aside.
2. Cut chicken in small cubes about ¾". Combine in a bowl with salt, sugar, sherry, soy sauce and honey. Marinate 1 hour.
3. Drain off marinade and reserve. Pat chicken dry with paper towels, dip in cornstarch and then in beaten egg.

4. Heat oil to 350° in deep skillet and brown walnuts in it.
5. Remove walnuts; brown chicken in same pan with ginger and garlic.
6. Add water, msg, bamboo shoots and the reserve marinade. Cover and simmer for 10 minutes. Add the walnuts and cook 1 minute more.
7. Cool to room temperature; cover and refrigerate.

**AT PARTY TIME:**
1. About 1 hour before serving, remove from refrigerator.
2. Reheat, either in electric frying pan set at 250° or in 250° oven for 10 minutes, until heated through.

# *Tim Sun Gnow*
## *(Sweet and Sour Beef)*

3 pounds sirloin or eye round
   steak, ½" thick
2 eggs, beaten
2 garlic cloves, minced
1½ cups cornstarch
1 cup peanut oil for frying
2 20-ounce cans pineapple
   chunks

3 cups water
½ cup dry sherry
1½ cups vinegar
1 cup sugar
2 teaspoons salt
2 packages frozen snow peas
1 box cherry tomatoes, hulled

**DAY BEFORE PARTY:**
1. Cut beef in ½" cubes. Mix eggs with garlic and dip meat in mixture. Roll meat in ½ cup of cornstarch.
2. Heat oil in electric frying pan to 375° and fry meat cubes 3 minutes until browned. Drain on paper towels. Discard all but 2 tablespoons oil.
3. Drain pineapple; save the juice. Mix remaining ½ cup cornstarch with pineapple juice; then blend in water, sherry, vinegar, sugar and salt. Cook in electric frying pan over low heat, stirring until thick.

4. Add pineapple and beef; cook 3 minutes.

5. Cool to room temperature; cover and refrigerate. (Snow peas, defrosted, and cherry tomatoes will be added just before serving.)

**AT PARTY TIME:**

1. Remove beef-pineapple mixture from refrigerator 1 hour before serving.

2. In electric skillet or oven set at 250°, reheat beef for 10 minutes or until heated through. Test for seasoning. Add peas and cherry tomatoes and cook 3 minutes more.

## *For Toi Chow Fan*
### *(Precious Fried Rice)*

2½ teaspoons salt
2½ cups raw rice
6 tablespoons peanut oil
  for frying
¾ cup sliced pork sausage
  or bacon
1 cup diced cooked Virginia
  ham
½ cup shredded cooked
  chicken
2 cups cooked shrimp, diced
1 package snow peas,
  defrosted
10 water chestnuts, minced
3 eggs, well beaten

*Sauce:* mix together
1 cup soy sauce
3 tablespoons sherry
1 teaspoon salt
½ teaspoon white pepper
1½ tablespoons cornstarch

**DAY BEFORE PARTY:**

1. Bring 5½ cups water to a boil; add salt and rice; lower heat

and simmer, covered, for 25 minutes or until all water is absorbed. Refrigerate overnight.

2. Prepare sauce and refrigerate.

**ABOUT TWO HOURS BEFORE SERVING:**

1. Add 3½ tablespoons cold water to cold rice to loosen grains.

2. Heat oil in frying pan to 350°. Fry bacon or sausage for 2 minutes, stirring constantly.

3. Add ham, chicken, shrimp, and sauce. Cook for 2 minutes.

4. Add rice and cook for 2 more minutes, stirring constantly. Set aside, covered, at room temperature.

**JUST BEFORE SERVING:**

1. Reheat rice mixture for 3 or 4 minutes. Add snow peas, water chestnuts, and eggs. Stir constantly until all ingredients are thoroughly mixed. Cook for 2 minutes and serve.

# *Jow Mein*
## *(Fried Noodles)*

4 5-ounce cans chow mein fried noodles. (Serve at room temperature or heat for a few minutes in 250°–300° oven.)

# *Baak Fan*
## *(Steamed Rice)*

24 ounces (1½ pounds long grain rice)

**HALF AN HOUR BEFORE SERVING:**

Bring 7 cups of water to a boil, add 2 teaspoons salt and rice, cover and cook over low heat until water is absorbed and rice is tender.

# Jih Maah Baang
## (Sesame Seed Cookies)

2 cups sifted flour
1 teaspoon baking power
¼ teaspoon salt
1 stick of butter, softened

1 cup less 2 tablespoons sugar
1 egg
2 tablespoons toasted sesame
    seeds
2 tablespoons dry sherry

**ONE OR TWO DAYS BEFORE PARTY:**
1. Sift together flour, baking powder, and salt.
2. Cream butter and sugar, beat in egg and stir in sesame seeds. Blend in flour mixture alternately with the sherry. Chill dough 1 or 2 hours.
3. Preheat oven to 375°.
4. Drop chilled dough from teaspoon onto ungreased cookie sheets. Flatten to ⅛″ thickness with a glass. Bake until cookies are lightly browned around edges (about 10 minutes). (Makes 36 cookies.)

# Hung Yun Beang
## (Chinese Almond Cakes)

36 whole blanched almonds
2½ cups sifted flour
¾ cup sugar
¼ teaspoon salt
1 teaspoon baking powder
1½ sticks of butter

1 egg
1 teaspoon almond extract
1 egg yolk

**ONE OR TWO DAYS BEFORE PARTY:**
1. Blanch almonds by covering with boiling water. Let stand 5 or 10 minutes. Drain. Place in cold water. Slip off skins (if any). Drain on paper towels.

2. Sift flour with sugar, salt, and baking powder into large bowl.

3. Using pastry blender or 2 knives, cut in butter until mixture resembles cornmeal.

4. Beat egg with 3 tablespoons water and the almond extract. Add to flour mixture, mixing with fork until dough leaves side of bowl.

5. On lightly floured surface, knead dough until smooth. Wrap in waxed paper. Refrigerate 1 hour.

6. Preheat oven to 350°.

7. Form dough into 1″ balls. Place 3″ apart on ungreased cookie sheets.

8. With palm of hand, flatten each cookie to a circle about ¼″ thick. Press an almond into the center of each.

9. Combine egg yolk with 1 tablespoon water. Brush on cookies.

10. Bake 20 to 25 minutes or until golden. Remove to wire rack; let cool. Makes 36 cookies.

## *(Fortune Cookies)*

These traditional endings to a Chinese meal—at least as far as Americans are concerned—are not even known in China! In fact, Fortune Cookies were invented by Japanese immigrants on the West Coast, who first put messages in rice cakes. The rice cakes crumbled, so the inventive bakers devised the more sturdy dough used in fortune cookies as we know them. Since the messages are always up-key and pleasant, it's a nice touch to include them for a New Year party where everyone and everything should be happy. (Buy the cookies, already made, in supermarkets or specialty shops.)

## *Jasmine Tea*

You may have to borrow one or two glass teapots from friends in order to brew the 20-odd cups of tea needed for your party.

Always follow these directions when making "real" (not teabag) tea: First, rinse the teapot out with boiling water. Then add 1 teaspoon of tea for each cup, plus "one for the pot." Add appropriate cups of boiling water and let the tea steep for 2 to 5 minutes. (If tea is not going to be poured at once, transfer to another pre-warmed teapot and strain; the tea gets bitter if it sits too long.)

## *Expenses for Chinese New Year's Party for 18–24:*

| | |
|---|---|
| $24.00 | Shao Hsing Wine (8 16-ounce bottles) before and during dinner |
| 11.80 | Japanese Beer, Kirin ($2.95 a six-pack) with dinner |
| 12.05 | Yang Chow Haah Kow (fried shrimp balls) |
| 8.75 | Char Siu (cold pork with mustard sauce) |
| 12.70 | Shew Pye Gult (barbecued spareribs) |
| 4.50 | Yeung Doon Gwoo (stuffed mushrooms) |
| 5.95 | Chungun (spring rolls, egg rolls) |
| 1.15 | Bo-Pe (meat dumplings) |
| 6.45 | Haap to Ghuy (chicken with walnuts) |
| 8.30 | Tim Sun Gnow (sweet and sour beef) |
| 5.10 | For Toi Chow Fan (precious fried rice) |
| 2.60 | Jow Mein (fried noodles) (4 5-ounce cans) |
| .50 | Baak Fan (steamed rice) |
| .75 | Jih Maah Baang (sesame seed cookies) |
| 1.05 | Hung Yun Beang (almond cakes) |
| 1.00 | Fortune Cookies |
| 1.00 | Jasmine Tea |
| $107.60 | |

Celebrate "Kung Hsi" with 24 friends for less than $4.50 per person.

# Index

## Beverages

### Cocktails and aperitifs

## Sauces

## Soup

## Vegetables

### Vegetable hors d'oeuvres and appetizers

### Vegetable Main Course Accessories